Be Unmessable

Navigate Any Stressful Situation, Conversation, or Crisis

KAREN POHLMAN

Be Unmess le: Navigate any Stressful Situation, Conversation or Crisis

Published b Another Way Publishing LLC
San Jose, Ne Mexico

This book is eant to provide accurate and authoritative information regarding the subject tter covered. It is sold with the understanding that the publisher and author not engaged in rendering psychological or other professional services. If e ert assistance or counseling is needed, the services of a competent professional ould be sought.

Some name nd identifying details have been changed to protect the privacy of individuals.

ISBN: 978- 73-62943-0-7
SEL02700 ELF-HELP / Personal Growth / Success

Cover phot y Jordan Ashley Photography
Cover Desi by Laura Duffy
Interior desi by Victoria Wolf, wolfdesignandmarketing.com
Photos of M n Street house by unknown photographer, courtesy of Zillow.
Photos of P lman family by Karen and Brent Pohlman

QUANTI PURCHASES: Schools, companies, professional groups, clubs, and other o anizations may qualify for special terms when ordering quantities of is title. For information, email Karen@anotherway.live.

Printed in the United States of America.

To everyone who ever let circumstances or people get in the way of enjoying this one short life.

Contents

Introduction

IN 2008 I FOUND MYSELF HOMELESS—with three children, my husband, and our dog living in tents in the middle of the Coconino National Forest in Arizona—squatting over a hole I had for dug myself, literally. It was shortly after my fortieth birthday. How did I get there? My story is both common and ordinary, but also extraordinary.

I grew up in Morton Grove, a small middle-class suburb of Chicago, the youngest of three girls in an English family that had immigrated to America in 1961. My parents were pioneers, the first in their families to leave the UK, paving a new road for our family. I was the summer surprise of 1968 and the first in our family to be born in the US.

My mom was a compassionate, proper lady who always rooted for the underdog and wanted everyone to feel loved and her daughters to be strong. Growing up during World War II in England, she found her childhood home to be stressful, and she experienced some difficult traumas that she chose to turn into unconditional love. My dad was a soft-spoken, blue-collar gentleman who had worked and traveled with Rolls-Royce Motor Cars for twenty-five years and then shifted to owning his own business in Illinois in the seventies. He raised his three daughters to do everything a son could have done: cutting the grass, changing tires, and moving heavy items. My sisters and I grew up in that small suburban home with lots of love, a dose of craziness, and a whole lot of inner drive. After high school, energetic and ambitious, I worked alongside my sister Diane as a makeup artist and aesthetician at her chic day spa north of Chicago, on Lake Michigan's North Shore.

One night after work, I drove my twenty-one-year-old self down to my one-bedroom apartment on Division Street to have dinner with my sister Julie. But she had a change of plans, so my friends Lainey and Barrie took me out on the town. We ended up at a trendy, new nightclub in Fulton Market called The Shelter, which provided one of many examples in my life that proves God has a fantastic sense of humor. There wasn't much going on that night, and the manager bought us drinks so we would stay and hit the dance floor. In the time it took for us to down a round, a guy walked in and stood by the doorway, observing the scene. He was hot, stylish, and full of confidence in himself. He had arrived on a mission to find a date for the Billy Idol concert that Friday night in Alpine Valley. He found her. The year was 1990. Brent and I fell magnetically and wildly in love, and that is where my story begins.

What follows is a very real story of love and loss, faith and despair, bad times and amazing times. It is a story of intimacy, choice, and the human condition. It's also how we not only survive the dramas of life, but also use those experiences to grow, improve, and contribute. My story involves loss. We built our dream home with our own hands, only to be forced to give it up—when the global financial crisis hit in 2008—for that tent in the woods I mentioned earlier. We also lost each other for a six-month period in 1996 when we separated and I filed for divorce but didn't go through with it and a ten-month period in 2004 when we separated and then divorced. But my story also entails growth, as we were lucky enough to rediscover each other again and keep our family together through a tremendous crisis while developing a lens of gratitude for all we had been through. This abundance mindset later attracted the attention of producers from *The Ellen DeGeneres Show*, along with a $20,000 check, but more about that later.

Today, I am happy to say that I've been married and remarried to my soul mate and business partner for twenty-seven years, including the months we were apart in 1996 and in 2004. Like any people in a long-term relationship, we have had our share of challenges, and like all couples, we still do. Being who we are, we are now able to face any challenge and do our best to resolve it with what we have at the time, no matter how dramatic or chaotic. After years of facing life's challenges together, we still drive each other crazy at times, but we can't seem to live without each other.

This book, though, is not about marriage. It's about relationships in general and especially the one you have with yourself. I have been a person who was troubled and burdened by outside circumstances, allowing people and life to mess with me. The pain and suffering I experienced from this inadvertently caused me to hurt others with my short temper, critical judgments, and inability to be present. Hurting people, hurt others. I've also been a person who was around others who were burdened by outside circumstances, and it's been awful to have been around them sometimes. This book is about being courageous and learning how to face the adversity of life, with all its joys and sorrows, in a way that is resilient and steady. In a way that is good for you and good for others. Yes, I learned all of this in my own life, but what I learned in my life can work for you too. Just as I learned exactly who I was and what I was made of so I could get through the worst of times, so can you.

From your perspective, you may wonder why I put up with some of what I did, but from my perspective, I may wonder the same about you. My responses to adversity, uncertainty, and challenging times have ranged from terribly painful to liberating and enlightening. They have shaped me as a mom, a wife, a friend, a lover, a fellow human, and, most of all, as a passionate teacher of being "unmessable," which I roughly define as the ability to stand in the face of any circumstance and find possibility.

Most of all, I wrote this book to make sure that everyone in the world has access to the knowledge and process that it takes to become unmessable. Life is short, and my deepest desire is that people come to know how to stop letting other people and outside circumstances get them twisted in a bunch. That way they can get back to loving one another.

In part I of this book, I tell the story of how we lost everything and what came of it. Life has a funny way of showing its humor when it comes to how much we think we can plan and control, as life can be very uncertain and have its share of challenges. I've also assembled my hard-fought life lessons into a process I call "Live Another Way," which is described in part II. This process will empower you to become unmessable and handle whatever life may throw your way. Each chapter in part II has a "For Your Journal" section at the end, with exercises that will enable you to further reflect on each chapter. And the information you discover during your reflection will translate into your own unique way of utilizing the strategies to create your personalized unmessable process.

As I was assembling all the ideas I had for this process with my business coach Kim, attempting to condense my message down to fewer words, I heard her use the word "unmessable." At that moment, it stuck with me, and I began using unmessable to describe the type of resilience I had acquired from my experiences. I'll elaborate on this a bit more later.

Life will hand you unexpected trials, challenges and people that stretch you and push you into places you haven't been before. The strategies in this book will equip you to face life's dramas with courage and certainty that you will make it through. Practicing these strategies will improve your relationship with yourself, which translates into more fulfilling relationships with others and more joy, peace, and freedom in your life. Mastering these strategies will make you unmessable, and you'll come out the other side of challenges stronger and with more insight, knowledge, and opportunities.

Life is short; make the most of it today!

Jenn
xo

PART I

LOSING IT!

Chapter 1

DIGGING THE HOLE

LET'S BEGIN WITH THE STORY of how we lost everything. It was 2005. Brent and I had known each other for fifteen years—been married for twelve—and at that point we had been divorced and separated for ten months. The break brought about some essential perspective for us both, and we began chatting and spending time together, which lead to some much-needed counseling and eventual dating each other again. Then one night he came over after work while the kids were sleeping and asked if I wanted to work with him on a construction project we had briefly discussed—building a new house.

"Hey, I was thinking. How would you like to draw up the new house I showed you—for the property we found in Cary—and then live in it with me?"

"I don't want to live in such a big house."

"How come? It's going to be beautiful, like a museum."

"I'm nc ınto living in a museum. I want a regular, nice house with furniture—deco: ted to make it a home for our family."

"Don't ll me you don't like nice things; I know you do."

"I'm nc You're right. I do like nice things, but I don't want to live in a giant house

This co ersation played out a familiar pattern in our relationship, as we both tried t fill our own voids. It reminded me of a conversation we'd had in 1999, when e purchased our first home. We had found a supercute neighborhood near g at schools in Park Ridge, Illinois, close to O'Hare International Airport anc nly twenty minutes from downtown Chicago. It had a wonderful hometo ı feel and was a place where neighbors had cookouts and block parties and joyed life together. Real estate in that area was booming. People were buyin lder homes and either rehabbing them or tearing them down and buildin new and bigger houses on the existing lots. It was a hot area, and we knew th emodeling business well!

I was th lled that after six years of marriage, we were able to buy our first house. No r re moving from rental to rental. I could finally make it ours and more than a erile, generic rental with white walls. I had waited six years and was so excited to ıoose wall colors, drapes, and blinds and to pick out fun furnishings. I was also se n months pregnant with our third child by the time it was my first opportunit o really make a house into a home for my family, and I was elated! I was lookin forward to nesting with feelings I had never before experienced.

Brent v s also thrilled, but his vision for this house was different from mine. His w focused on how to maximize the property and use this house as a launching ıd for our remodeling business. He wanted to gut the house and update it fr ı the ground up. It was to be a showcase for our work!

His pla actually made sense to me, so I decided to put off my plan and go along wi his, even though it meant not standing up for what I needed. I didn't know t the time the effect that decision would have on our relationship or our grow g family, but I found out soon enough.

My mom had come into town from Florida for the birth of the baby. I had decided to have the baby at home with a midwife, so mom was already there helping out the morning after our daughter, Amethyst, was born. That morning she had been making breakfast for the kids and getting them to school when Brent started, literally, breaking ground in the basement. Mom quietly came into my room whispering.

"Karen. Karen, I just want you to know Brent is in the basement banging. Is that OK?"

I opened my eyes, turned over in bed and looked at her to say, "Mom, that's fine. Just let him go."

That was the start of a three-and-a-half-year grueling remodeling project. It was a huge renovation. We gutted that house, but not all at once. We didn't have all the money up front, so we did it piecemeal on the weekends and in between paying-customer projects. We lived in the project, on the job site, with our kids. They grew up on the job site. It was a constant mess, with various areas of the house ripped apart and half completed as we transformed our small, two-bedroom bungalow into a giant Frank Lloyd Wright-style house. My life was a never-ending attempt to keep up with the mess, the needs of the kids, the needs of my husband, the business, and the house. Not only wasn't I being true to myself, but also there was always so much going on that I didn't have the time to figure out what I really wanted or needed. Back then I also didn't have the emotional vocabulary or communication skills to know what to ask for or to be able to do it even if I knew it.

Our neighbors thought we were crazy. The house was the talk of the block, and Brent would often invite people over to come see the next new cool thing we were working on. I must admit that I did enjoy the accolades we received for living through this crazy project and even acted like I was totally OK with everything, but inside I knew I wasn't. The truth was that I was depressed and falling apart. Living in that mess, with its accompanying financial strain and uncertainty of a completion date, was very challenging for me.

I had a void that I was trying to fill. I really wanted a home to raise our kids in and celebrate holidays and birthdays, to make memories that would last our lifetimes, and it became instead a nightmare project that threatened to go on forever. I honestly thought that having a decorated, furnished home would fill that void, and the thought of having it only made me more resentful the longer it took to get. I lived in a constant state of overwhelming anxiety and hopelessness and blamed my husband for all these feelings of frustration, anger, and sadness.

By the time we did finish the house, our youngest child, Amethyst, was four years old, and our marriage was in turmoil. His idea was to celebrate the fact that we had finally completed the project, and I couldn't bear to show up at the show up place. I was still hyperfocused on the fact that we still didn't have the home that I had wanted.

Fighting about it, I yelled at him, "Yeah, but we don't even have furniture!"

"You sound so materialistic. . . . I can't believe that all you can focus on is the fact that we don't have furniture now."

So, back to our 2005 conversation, I felt a strong déjà vu and didn't want to repeat the previous construction nightmare.

I asked him, "What if we spend all this time and money on building a big house and then don't have enough money to fill it with furniture? That's important to me."

I could feel his discomfort. It was palpable. It wasn't about him; my questioning was about me and having a comfy life and the home I wanted for our family.

"Can you imagine yourself in that beautiful home when it's done? It'll be awesome. We'll have a rec room for the kids where they can bring all their friends to hang out at our house. We'll have space for family parties and having friends over. It'll be great! You'll love it!"

I truly wanted to believe that this new house he was describing could be the same home I had always wanted for my family. This may have been because I was two years on the path of my personal development journey and felt like

I had figured out a bunch of my stuff and could see we were finally getting along really well. I wanted to believe this house would be our family's legacy home and that if I put in more time and effort, it would be the family home I dreamed about. This was the chance for our relationship to heal and begin again fresh. I figured it was meant to be.

So I believed.

Our marriage was exciting from the beginning, but also hot-tempered. We brought three beautiful children into this world over the first six years of marriage while we struggled with our own parent-child relationship, I was the child and Brent was the parent. Those early years were overwhelming for me—learning the construction business, having babies, adjusting to a new marriage, and trying to keep business finances in order. Even though a part of me knew I had needs that weren't being met, there wasn't time for me and my needs. Had I been more equipped at the time or had a coach to show me the way, I would have made space to address what I needed. I was hungry for guidance, but I didn't have any.

This left me stuck in a "blame game" mode toward my husband without the personal skills needed to successfully navigate all I was facing. I had fallen in love with his big ideas and "I don't care what you think" attitude, but what I really desired was his gentle side, reassuring me that I was loved and valuable. We fought a lot, and I often worried that I had married the wrong guy.

Chapter 2

HOME SWEET HOME

AFTER TEN YEARS OF RELATIONSHIP STRUGGLE, numerous near breakups, makeups, and mess-ups, Brent decided he didn't want to be married to me anymore and moved out. Being alone was a wake-up call. Though it was terrifying, it also made me realize that I had better do something, or I stood to lose the family I had lovingly spent ten years creating. That was the point when I began that personal development journey through which I found the deeper spiritual connection I had always longed for.

I started by joining a women's support group at a local church and enlisted the help of a licensed family counselor named Brenda, whom I had found on a referral list at the church. At first, I felt stupid when I owned up to the stuff that was actually going on in my head and heart. For months when my counselor would ask me how I felt, I would answer, "I don't know. I'm pissed and angry." I didn't have a broad emotional vocabulary at that time. I was in a place where seemed I knew nothing, and I felt so helpless and ashamed that it took mar ge struggles to wake me up.

After B nt left, I had the time I needed to sort it all out, and it worked. The renewed sp tual connection I finally achieved gave me a feeling of certainty, love, and p pose that I had never known before. I was convinced that we would even ally reunite because why would God bring us together only to have it end, ght?

The div ce was finalized in 2004. But his 2005 phone call while he was out of the c ntry vacationing with the kids got us talking. The chitchat and light conve tion about what they had all been up to sparked the old flame in my heart an took me back to the fun times we'd had. Our conversation was light and ea , bordering on flirtatious. We rekindled our joy of being together in those co ersations, and it helped to turn a corner in our relationship.

That wi er, upon his return home from the vacation, he came over to my house one n ht asking to chat. He told me that his counselor, Cyndi, thought it would rea help the kids if we could get on the same page. He wasn't making any promis about us but asked if I would be open to going to counseling together. I a eed. In fact, this was exactly my desire prior to our divorce. I had hoped also at a counselor would get him to quit pointing the finger at me all the time his seemed like exactly what would get us back together, and if it didn't wo , at least it would make us better parents.

It wor d! I moved into the house with Brent and the children on Londonde St., and that spring we found the property that would be the site of that , beautiful house we talked about living in. We then inaugurated plans for a mazing French château on a little over a half-acre, with scenic views of the x River. It would be our family's dream home, which we lovingly referred to "Main Street."

Main eet was located near both of our original families. Parents, siblings, au , uncles, and even a ninety-four-year-old grandmother were all within a sh drive. It was also close to our church. Coffee chats, parties, and get-togethers were a consistent way of life for years, and Main Street was the perfect place to have more of those get-togethers and call our home.

It was the home I dreamed of, where our three children—Jade, Cole, and Amethyst—would grow to be productive adults, grow lifelong friendships, and pass through essential life milestones. It would be the place of memorable family gatherings, weddings, and reunions and where we would entertain friends and business associates. It was to be a legacy home to be passed down in the family over generations to come.

We spent countless hours planning and building that home. Many evenings after the kids went to bed, we discussed where we wanted particular rooms, down to where the plumbing and electrical outlets would be. We talked about how best to build it and how it would all be laid out from the ground up. We also spent hours and hours picking out kitchen appliances, finishes and fixtures, cabinets, granite patterns, drawer and sink placement—down to how tall the faucets should be in order to clear appliances and allow unobstructed views of the great room to enable great conversations. We discussed everything in minute detail, details that made that house our amazing and wonderful and perfect family home.

All of this was discussed after full days of working our construction business, after feeding the kids dinner, and after discussing our twice-weekly counseling sessions. It was like our evening shift. Most of our time that wasn't spent working or taking care of our kids went to talking, discussing, planning, and strategizing this dream home. I'd sit at my drafting table with rulers, protractors, and drafting paper to pencil by hand the building plans for city permits while Brent would call out ideas and layouts for walls, windows, chimneys, and mechanicals.

Thousands of hours were given up for this home—time that could have been spent on date nights with each other, time with our children, time with our friends and family. It never occurred to us that we might be trying to fill a void or repeating our past—we were too busy focusing on building for our future.

We also solicited lots of input from family, friends, and our employees.

Even our ki played a part. During their summer break, Brent took time to teach them bout working for money while stocking the house with tile. We imported a hole semi of handmade Saltillo tiles from Mexico. We told our kids that if ey helped carry the tiles from the truck to the room where they were to be i talled, we would pay them each a flat rate of $500. The plan was that Jade ar Cole would carry three tiles at a time and Amethyst only one. They even de it into a game, sometimes racing one another up the stairs. They worke happily, singing and joking around with one another. They even noticed litt animal footprints scattered on the tiles throughout the load, evidence th had probably been laid out to dry in the sun. It took several weeks, but ey got it done and each earned $500. It was a huge undertaking that we dec ed to make into a fun family project.

The ho was designed as a three-story French country estate with stucco walls and sla like tiles. It overlooked the river. It was 6,500 square feet and housed six bedroom six bathrooms, three fireplaces, two balconies, a five-car garage, and radiant-heat floors throughout the entire home. The custom kitchen was decorated with c inets fashioned by the Amish and countertops with granite from Brazil. The oms were framed with hand-hewn wooden beams on the ceilings, custom-ma cedar doors, and floors graced with imported Saltillo tiles. It even had a perso elevator to carry people between the three levels.

Bespoke tchen cabinets made by the Amish and Brazilian granite countertops.

Between 2005 and 2007, we worked our asses off running our business and putting our hearts and souls into creating our dream home. By the spring of 2007, we had moved in while we finished up working on the details. The kids stayed busy with school and camp in the summer. Jade played soccer, Cole played baseball, and Amethyst tagged along with me to these activities. We were in our late thirties, and life was good.

Then life changed. The financial crisis hit, banks were no longer lending money freely, and we felt the tightening of our belts. Then some of our clients stopped paying their bills. This was new territory to us because there had never been a problem collecting from customers. It got worse. A job to excavate a foundation for a new barn, a $100,000 job, ended in the payment never materializing. Construction lending halted, and projects were curtailed. One day Brent confided in a local construction guy and asked him if he was experiencing the same financial crunch. The guy said that he was and jokingly told Brent that if he was us, he'd fill the barn foundation hole back in.

We hadn't changed anything, but it was clear that not only had something outside our control definitely changed, but also we hadn't seen it coming and had no way to avoid it. The 2008 global financial crisis had arrived. The faucet had shut off and all income had halted.

Nonetheless, we kept working on the house, which meant spending more money, all the while foolishly thinking that if we worked harder or faster to finish, we could get it reappraised and remortgaged and live off the equity until things got going again. But that didn't happen.

Pohlman family home on Main Street

The wh le market crashed, and I was initially in denial. My response was to finis up on the punch lists and go back to the bank. We had never experienced market crash and had no idea what to expect or how to handle its fallout. A we knew was that we were quickly running out of money. Even though I w scared and confused, I was dangerously optimistic and figured everything ould be fine.

We con cted the mortgage guys who had once been so friendly when trying to ge our business. They had raked in the commissions from selling no-docume tation mortgages, mortgages that required no income verification from he borrower. The guys couldn't help us because banks weren't lending. W alked to people who might consider investing—no luck. We even thoug about selling the house, but no matter which way we turned, we couldn't ake a deal. We had sunk so much money, time, and effort into the house t, with the market change, the house cost way more than the neighborh d could support. The mortgage was upside down—we owed more on th house than we could sell it for. I was terrified and angry. I felt like we wer crewed!

After all we had been through in our marriage, how could God let this happen? It wasn't supposed to end like this. But that's exactly what was happening.

Nighttime, after the kids went to bed, was an awful time. It's when we had no choice but to sit down and figure out what to do. I wanted no part of it. I only wanted to be held and reassured that everything would turn out OK. I reasoned that these discussions were all just talk and options, not decisions. We didn't share anything with the kids at that point.

Then Brent spoke the cold, hard truth: "Karen we're not going to be able to keep the house. We're going to have to file bankruptcy and let the bank foreclose on the house."

Then in his next breath he said, "If we have to start over, then I don't want to live in a gray, sh*tty place. Let's find someplace sunny."

This was all too much for me. Inside I was dying and needing comfort. It was my worst nightmare coming true. I was blindsided, and he wanted to press on. I understood he was in problem-solving mode, but I was trying to cope with tremendous uncertainty, disbelief, and confusion. I still didn't know how to ask for what I wanted. In fact, not only did I not know what I wanted or needed, but I was also frozen. On one hand I knew I wanted to finish the house and decorate it and make it home, but I also didn't want him to experience me as being unsupportive, an old wound. So I pressed on. My heart was breaking.

To top it off, at that point I didn't know anyone else who was affected as we were with this financial crisis. I felt like we were the only ones and felt tremendous shame that we weren't able to make this project work out. I was like a walking zombie, dead inside and still moving forward.

Brent had a solution. He reasoned that if we had to survive on just a little money for a while, we could do it camping.

Camping? I figured it wouldn't be so bad since there were a bunch of great campgrounds we could find.

Brent countered with reality. "We won't be staying in a campground; we'll need to stay in tents on a simple campsite; tent camping is free." That's the only way we were able to make it work financially.

I didn't expect that, and it changed everything in my head. I was weighed down by the thought that this dream home attempt had failed, foreclosure might be in our future, and we were talking about living in tents with no water or electricity. But I couldn't think of another solution. All five of us living with a relative or potentially splitting up the family was not an option for us, and I still didn't want to live in a tent with my family of five (with our dog).

So, in the spirit of thinking outside the box, we came together to work out what we needed to do. If it was camping, well, it would be in a place that was close to where we wanted our family to write our next chapter.

We spent hours researching "Best Places to Live in the US" online and kept detailed notes. Among the things we valued were a solid economy, great schools, clean air, culture, great restaurants, and of course, mild weather with lots of sunshine. We settled on a few potential places: Florida, North Carolina, and northern Arizona. After more days of research, discussions, and prayers, we agreed on northern Arizona as our number-one pick. Florida had too many mosquitos and was too humid. North Carolina had good camping sites, but children were required to attend schools in the districts in which they lived, and the schools we liked weren't near those good camping sites. Northern Arizona had free camping in the national forest, sunny and dry weather, no bugs, and charter schools that were open to children regardless of where they lived. And close by, in Flagstaff, there was a highly rated charter school.

We made an initial plan. We'd camp for free until I found a job and then take it from there. Brent jumped right into "go mode" and handled logistics, like dealing with the fact that we wouldn't be able to keep all our belongings. We didn't have any income at that point, and storing a container would be a monthly cost. We could only get one. We would have a container delivered to the house and pack it with as much as we could, and the rest would be sold or given away. This is when we learned which things were important and which were just things.

But it's a whole different ballgame when you have to tell your kids that they can only keep a few of their things in the storage container. The whole family had to share this container, and we could only take a couple of things with us in the car. It was eating me up, but again I put this conversation off for another day.

Chapter 3

GOD'S COUNTRY

THINGS WERE MOVING WAY TOO QUICKLY. I wanted to slow the freight train down. I couldn't go forward and dismantle my life and my home without knowing if this was the right decision. I kept thinking about the situation and praying to God. I kept asking myself and God, Is this really what we should do? Is there someone we can live with maybe? Could the church help us with the mortgage payment so we wouldn't have to leave? I even asked Brent to go with me and ask for help at our church. We filled out its intake form, met with a church aid representative, and bared our souls while getting super vulnerable about our situation, but we were denied and advised to visit the food pantry. Again, I felt that familiar pain of being shocked and humiliated.

Exhausted, I finally realized this situation was way bigger than I had once thought. My dangerous optimism made me think that things were going to change somehow on their own. I was completely out of control.

Brent insisted, "Karen, you need to snap out of this and get your head out of the sand. There is no fixing this. We have to make a move before we implode!"

I was furious on the inside, thinking "What the f*ck!" But I was void of emotion on the outside. I was using every strategy I learned from the last two years of counseling to keep my temper and angry outbursts in check. I knew I needed to snap out of it. Trouble was, I didn't know how to snap out of it! My heart and brain felt like they were having a nuclear meltdown! I wanted a cooldown as soon as possible.

Wishful thinking. It was more like full steam ahead. Over the following weeks, moves were made, bankruptcy papers were signed, cars were repossessed, a PODS container was ordered, tents and sleeping bags were purchased, and the school year was brought to an end. Jade attended her eighth-grade graduation at Cary Junior High. Amethyst and Cole had no idea what we were planning, but Jade was old enough and observant enough to realize something was going on. The dread of telling them haunted me. We had moved so many times already in their short lives, and I hadn't planned on moving again. My heart was breaking for them. They were going to have to move away from friends again. I felt distressed and guilty. I was overwhelmed, thinking I was seriously screwing up my children's lives.

Once school ended for the summer, together we told the kids we were moving. Brent framed it this way: "Get excited because we are going to start over where there's clean air and it's sunny every day. We're going to live on a mountain, and it's going to be so cool!"

The kids were initially sad at the news and understandably confused, asking "Why do we have to move, Mom?"

I can't remember exactly what I told them but do remember trying to explain that sometimes things don't work out the way we want, and parents have to make tough decisions. I do remember feeling sick to my stomach, though.

I was proud of my kids. They were resilient and strong. They pulled out all their clothes and toys and belongings in their rooms, and we sorted through them all. We put things in piles of give away, keep for later, and keep for the road trip. I was sad watching them and helping them make difficult decisions at such a tender age about what they cared about and what they didn't mind throwing away. Again, I was angry inside that we were even in this situation. I was pissed that I ever agreed to build this house. In my gut I knew somehow it wasn't going to work out. I was so mad at Brent that we built such a big house even though I went along with it. I questioned whether we would be in this situation if we hadn't built it so big.

When we finally packed up the container, the kids wanted to know when they would get their stuff back.

"I don't know exactly" I said.

Then came the kicker: "Are we going to get our stuff back, Mom?"

I assured them they would, but inside my head I was thinking I wasn't so sure.

I couldn't give them a date because I had no idea, and I didn't want them to look forward to it only to be disappointed if it didn't happen, or worse, feel like they couldn't trust what I said.

Eventually, after Brent painted them an amazing mental picture of adventure, campfires every night, and roasting marshmallows, the kids met his enthusiasm. Because we had moved around a bunch when they were younger, pivoting came more easily to them.

I, on the other hand, was dealing with megauncertainty, loss of control, major shame, disappointment, and resentment. I was grieving the loss of everything I had put into that house. It was so much more than just a house. It was our legacy home, what I had always wanted and was so close to getting. It was like letting go of a child that I had given birth to. I was devastated and overwhelmed. I had put my all into it and now felt like I had been pounded into the ground.

The house we built was amazing. I put off spending time with friends and family, sacrificed vacations, and put off doing things so I could have a home to furnish and decorate and enjoy with my family and friends. Apparently, though, it wasn't meant to be.

We had said our goodbyes to friends and family over the previous weeks. I shared little with most of them, out of my need to hide from the shame I felt, telling most people that we were moving and going to camp for a while. On a summer day in June 2008, we left Main Street. On that departure day, my sister-in-law, Kari, niece Bryar, and cousin Max met us over at the house. None of us knew when we would see one another again, emotions were high, and tears were flowing. The kids were not only cousins; they were best friends. They had that kind of relationship in which they could get dropped off to play at any time. It was an amazing friendship in which they explored the outdoors together, climbed trees, built forts, and made up games and songs. They had a bond that was unbreakable, and the loss they felt that day was deep. They stood in our driveway waving at the five of us while we, along with our dog, pulled out in our rented Chevy Impala that we had paid for one month in advance. We waved back goodbye.

With a total of $2,200 in our bank account, we headed west on our 1,675-mile journey to a God-knows-where campsite in northern Arizona. After we found our way to the main highway, there was silence in the car; the kids were busy listening to music through shared ear buds on Jade's iPod Shuffle that her Auntie Julie had bought her, Brent was driving, and I was pretending we were off on a vacation. I sat in the passenger seat quietly thinking, "God help me." All I could do was sit and pray until I finally fell asleep.

It didn't take long for Brent to feel relief from no longer having to figure out how to come up with the $42,000 every month to make payroll, pay material suppliers and handle equipment leasing, bank mortgages, and our personal expenses just to break even. He was able to compartmentalize the situation and figured he just needed to look for the next opportunity to make money. For me, it was all one big emotional ball of crap. And whenever he mentioned how happy he was about it, I felt like strangling him.

I felt completely overwhelmed, with three children looking to us to keep their lives normal, safe, and happy while I had the additional pressure of keeping my own feelings of disappointment and shame hidden. Normal life for me ended abruptly that day. We were officially homeless, and I was a ticking time bomb.

A Rand McNally road atlas helped us find our way to a rest stop in Parks, Arizona. We arrived at night, and when we opened our doors and looked up at the sky, all we could see was millions of stars. It was spectacular! As tired as we were from the long drive, smiles were on all our faces as we looked in awe at the fantastic sight.

We slept in the car until the sun came up. In the morning, after brushing our teeth in the restroom, we headed into town to the ranger station to get a national forest map and figure out where to go next. Brent had confirmed with the rangers that we could set up a primitive campsite for our tents wherever we wanted as long as we set up a circle of rocks around the campfire and drowned out any fires we made. National forest rules stated that no person could camp longer than fourteen days in a month-long period, but the ranger told us that as long as we moved spots after fourteen days, most likely no one would notice—not enough staff. This wasn't going to be a KOA or Jellystone Park campsite with electricity, running water, and a concrete pad with a picnic table. We were roughing it.

Brent hiking around the camping area.

The forest roads were just dirt roads, and our Chevy Impala was no 4x4. It was sketchy, to say the least, as we drove that rental car back into the forest on the dirt roads, attempting to avoid big rocks and getting stuck in the ruts. We located a spot where someone else had camped before. It already had the rock circle for our campfire, and a spot had been cleared for the tents. This would be our new life for the next two weeks, before we had to move again.

The reality that this was our home for the time being set in fast for me as I looked around at the forest of ponderosa pines and saw that there was nothing else—no family, no friends, no couch, no refrigerator, no shower, no carpet, no bed, no thermostat or air conditioning, and no toilet. I was an accidental explorer. I hadn't asked to be there, but I was there. It was surreal. I pushed down my scared feelings and got on with setting up camp. The kids, on the other hand, couldn't wait to get out of the car and hike in the woods.

After we set up the three two-man tents and hoisted our cooler filled with food and ice over a tree branch to keep it out of reach of bears, we went for a short hike to see what was around. It was more forest; go figure. The Coconino National Forest encompasses approximately 1.8 million acres. Seeing other people was unlikely. We were on our own, and my momma bear instincts had been shifted into high gear.

Amethyst and Jade shared a tent, Cole and our dog, Quiggy, shared a tent, and Brent and I shared a tent. Our few belongings, such as clothes, stayed mostly in the trunk of the car. Other items—such as card games, books, and toys—went into the tents with the kids. Good night hugs and kisses were given in their tents while the kids snuggled into their sleeping bags on camping pads with their little battery-operated lanterns nearby. Then we headed off to our space. The laughing and talking of the girls could easily be heard through the thin nylon tent walls. Darkness and no electronic devices coupled with fresh air put the children to sleep easily.

Brent and I had our alone time in the tent. Fooling around changed a bunch, as sound traveled easily in the dead quiet, and the last thing I felt like doing was getting it on; I blamed him for everything. Tent time at night also became time to talk about our adult problems: how much money was left; my fears about bears, wolves and other campers; getting the kids enrolled in time for school; and finding work.

That first night was terrifying for me even though I had camped many times in my life. It was so dark! I would rather have held my bladder all night than venture outside the tent. When I first heard the coyotes, it sounded like a pack of thirty wolves. I didn't know what they were, and they seemed so close. I was completely freaked out! I made Brent move the car closer to the tents in case I needed to shuttle the children inside it to save them. Brent kept telling me that the dog would hear something before we would and warn us if any animals were too close to the tents. That didn't relieve any of my anxiety!

I was having a tough time over the next few weeks. I missed my friends, my women's group, my sisters, my family. I missed my life. My social life was gone, and I expected Brent to meet all my needs, an impossible task to expect of another person. A life that had once been filled with thriving relationships and social c ings was taken away, and I was devastated. It left a huge hole in my life that struggled to fill.

We hac o jobs and lots of time on our hands, so many of our waking hours were ent thinking how we could change our situation. We spent hours and hours e ry day talking about what we could do and discussing where we would go to nd work and how to find our next "lily pad." I was exhausted. This situation se ned impossible to get out of, and I felt completely overwhelmed with the pr ure of resolving it.

I also w nted to be present for the kids and at the same time be supportive and pres nt for Brent. His method of coping with difficult situations was through lot f discussion, communication, strategizing, and an exhaustingly large amou of thinking. My brain was getting a crash course in such thinking that summe f 2008. It was all too much for me, with no opportunity to take a break and n time for myself. No one was taking care of me, and I was terrible at self-care. us, I couldn't even enjoy the camping aspect because this wasn't camping to ne. There was no end date to this ordeal; we were homeless.

A week nto the experience, after spending about one third of our money on gasoline nd food, we were in town going to The Home Depot, and we had a conv sation about getting jobs. Brent noticed a Hiring Now sign for the hot og hut outside Home Depot and suggested I check it out. This sugges on brought up old wounds I was holding onto for too long. Three years nto our marriage, our business faced financial challenges, and I suggested h get a full-time job, which he did for three months, hated, and went back being self-employed. Later, if I ever suggested getting a job again, he re used.

In my t gered state, I exploded, "Are you f*cking kidding me? Why don't you get the b at the hot dog stand?"

Then h eminded me: "Karen, remember discussing you were going to get a full-ti job, and I was going to work on building a business? We need money righ way."

"I know we do! And I'm still not going to apply for a job at the hot dog stand! I'll find something else!" In my fragile state, I couldn't bear to apply for a minimum wage job and, for some reason, not get it. That would have thrown me over the edge. My identity was definitely wrapped up in my vocation, and I didn't want to be a forty-year-old hot dog girl. Not that there's anything wrong with that; it just wasn't an option for me. I was willing to gamble there was a job more in line with my skills somewhere in my near future.

Transitioning from challenging moments like that one to showing up for the kids or moving onto other things that needed my attention was difficult, as I felt like my brain was hijacked. I prayed to God and asked what I should do. All I heard from God was "love him." Making phone calls to my friends Beth and Edna in Chicago to vent or writing letters to God on my computer to dump all the trash talk out of my head gave me the brain space to change my focus and show up for my family. I felt heard, validated, and loved by my friends. Once my cup was filled with love from friends and faith, I was able to pour out love to my family again.

The kids spent their days exploring the area, playing games they made up in the forest such as pinecone wars. They also read books while sitting in the sunshine, journaled by the campfire, and acted like goofy kids. Cole built forts with the sticks he found and created art statues with stacked rocks. The girls listened to music, sang songs, and made up dances. I was relieved; they actually seemed to be thriving. It was such a joy to see them playing, laughing, and having such a great time with one another.

Amethyst and Jade playing around at the campsite.

Afternoons during July and August brought monsoons, and sometimes we'd go to the local library or bookstore to get out of the rain and use an actual toilet. I felt really conspicuous when we'd go into a store or a coffee shop because we didn't spend money there. We were there only to use the restroom. It felt like everyone knew our situation, and I was embarrassed.

In the forest, having a toilet meant hiking out a little way away from the "living space," digging a little hole under the pine needles on the forest floor with the small spade, squatting, aiming, taking care of business, and covering it up with the dirt that was removed. We learned fast about the importance of having really good balance. Otherwise, it was pine needles in the butt cheeks. Quick, efficient, and clean was the way to be. However, we never forgot to visit a real bathroom whenever we were in town.

After two and a half weeks of living this new life, we met a guy at the Galaxy Diner we had heard about through a mutual friend. He was in the process of moving to Flagstaff for a new chief executive position. We ate lunch together and got to know him. He said that he needed to hire an assistant for his new position, and after some conversation about what sort of business we'd owned over the last fifteen years, he hired me on the spot. I started work a couple of weeks later.

The relief of finally getting a job was exciting until I remembered that all of my work clothes were packed away in the PODS container that was in storage. I had no clothes and no money to buy new ones, so I went to Kohl's department store and applied for its credit card and was approved for $300. I felt like God was on my side and was elated that I didn't have to spend the money out of pocket. I bought three easy-care work dresses and a pair of black heels. Every few days we would visit the laundromat on Milton Street, get coins from the dollar changer, and wash our clothes. We didn't have hangers or a closet in the forest. Most of our clothes were either kept in duffle bags or folded and stored in a basket in the trunk of the rental car.

Getting ready for work became an experience for me since we didn't have a bathroom or even a basic kitchen to easily prepare breakfast. We did have an Igloo cooler, paper plates, plasticware, and a little space to store food, so cereal with milk and PB&J sandwiches became the breakfast of champions.

Showering, something else we had taken for granted, became a luxury. A couple of times we visited a local truck stop's facility and purchased shower time at $10 per shower, which wasn't in our budget. We began filling up water jugs at the gas station spigot or wherever we could get free water. Before work, I'd boil some water in our only pan on a hot plate powered by a small propane tank and mix it with cool water from our blue storage jugs in an orange Home Depot five-gallon bucket. Brent helped me shower. I would stand naked by the side of the car, where I was blocked from the kids' eyesight while he slowly poured the warm water over my head. I would have to soap up quickly while standing in the cool morning mountain breeze. I couldn't lather much because there wouldn't be enough water to rinse it off. After the final rinse, I'd dry off with a towel and slip on one of my Kohl's dresses and put my makeup on using the mirror on the visor of the car.

The only potential giveaway to coworkers that we were living in a primitive campsite was that as soon as I was done rinsing off, my feet would get muddy. I took care of this by getting to the office early, wearing flip-flops and rinsing my feet off- ne foot at a time—in the bathroom sink. I'd then dry them with the hand dr r, slip into my office shoes, toss my flip-flops into a bag under my desk, and b in the workday. No one was the wiser.

As I m tioned earlier, one of the draws to Arizona was that we didn't need to live n district" for our kids to go to school in that district. As long as we drove th children to school, we could live anywhere in the state, and we wanted our ds to go to this great charter school in Flagstaff. Charter schools in Arizona considered public schools and are mostly free, with a few minor fees. This al gave us a broader choice for finding a house to rent.

We we able to get Jade and Cole onto the charter school waiting list, but Jade wa uite a few people down the list and Cole was even further down the list, so also initially registered them for other schools. We registered Jade at Flag ff High School with the hope that she would eventually get into Northland eparatory Academy. No one knew we were homeless. We filled out the sch l forms with the address of the local Mail Boxes Etc. suite box that we pur ased when we arrived in town.

Karen iles after moving into the family's first house after living in the woods.

With a stroke of luck, good timing, lots of prayers, and an advance from my new boss, we rented a house on Harmony Lane. It happened in late August, just before school started. Jade was able to ride the bus to the public high school, and Brent could drop me off at work before taking Cole and Amethyst to their wonderful Montessori charter schools, which were also free to the public. It seemed like everything was coming together beautifully.

We settled into our new home. It had amazing views since it was situated at the base of the San Francisco Peaks near Arizona Snowbowl, the local ski hill. It was set on an acre of land overlooking a beautiful meadow, and the kids loved playing outside, finding horny toads and hummingbirds, and pretending they were still camping by cooking pancakes over an open fire in the yard. I was able to work during the day and come home to a real house with a real toilet, shower after work, and help the kids with their homework.

Jade, Amethyst, and Cole on their first day of school after living in the woods. San Francisco Peaks in the background.

We didn't have furniture yet, as our container was still in storage. We set up our camping pads and sleeping bags in our new rooms and kept our clothes on the clos floor. We filled the kitchen cabinets with our plasticware and paper plate We went grocery shopping since we finally had a refrigerator. It was our nev ome. Life was beginning to feel more normal.

Then a uple of weeks later the unexpected happened. We found mold in the hous and Brent insisted we move out right away to avoid any more strain on ou immune systems. We did get our deposit back, but because it was August a college town, most of the rentals were already taken so we had to go b k to the forest until we could find another. This time we set up a camp j t off of Snowbowl Road on a Forest Service road. After going through th rocess of setting up a whole new campsite, we realized that we couldn't all ower with buckets in the morning before school and work, so we bought three-month membership to the local community center, the Flagstaff Ac aplex, and rented a storage unit for our clothes and other items we couldn't eave in the tents during the day. We put all the things that we didn't need ght away in the back of the storage unit and set up a rod in the front for ha ging clothes. We arrived at the community center, and unlike most patro who arrived with gym bags, we only carried clothes and a towel. Jade questic ed whether people knew that we were homeless.

Jade's first day at Flagstaff High School.

Imagine how challenging that was for our fourteen-year-old daughter—being a freshman and being homeless. Not only did she keep this a secret from people at school, but somehow she had the wherewithal to navigate being the new kid in school and adapting to the small-town way of life. Like me, she didn't want people knowing that she was showering at the community center with her family, no workout included.

One day I was on my crappy Google phone with my mother-in-law, Carol, blubbering to her about what a hard time I was having. She was awesome at letting me vent on that day, and she asked me,

"Have you thanked God for what he is doing for you?"

"Ugh, no. I forgot to"

That was the turning point for me. Life wasn't happening to me; it was happening for me. Her reminder sparked me to wake up and be grateful for all that I had, even though it wasn't exactly the way I wanted it. We still had so much to be grateful for: the love of family; the roof, albeit thin, over our heads; and the gift of still having most of our basic needs met.

At that point we came to a conclusion, as a family, that we weren't homeless, we were houseless. We had in fact created a loving home wherever we wound up, whether in a French château, our rental car, or a group of tents in the woods. It was the love that we shared, the relationships we created with one another, and the certainty of family that defined home to us. A house was just a building. The clarity of the saying "home is where the heart is" rang true for us.

Immediately, my perspective began to change, and over the next several weeks, I searched for opportunities to use what our experiences had taught us to help others. It was then that I began to dream about writing a book and sharing it with Oprah Winfrey or Ellen DeGeneres one day. I talked about this regularly with the family, and I even recorded a video on that Google phone, pretending to talk to Ellen as I sipped on a plastic cup of red wine at dusk in the woods. In my pretend interview, I told her that I was practicing being on her show so one day so I could tell her our success story.

This latest stint in the woods lasted for another four weeks before we found another house. This time we sent for our storage unit and set up our stuff in our new home. We were there for a year until the lease was up; then we upgraded to a larger house on the other side of town so the kids could each have their own room. This was important to us since Jade was now a sophomore in high school and needed alone time without her little sister always around.

Six months later, after settling into this new space, a knock at the door one day revealed that our landlord had been accepting our rent checks, but not paying his mortgage and the bank was foreclosing on the house we were renting. We had to move again! To top it all off, the company I was working for reorganized to a new location, my job was eliminated, and the business partner Brent was working with on their new venture, decided to go a different direction.

Brent and I realized that after trying to make ends meet in this small town, it still wasn't working like it needed to, and we weren't going to have enough money to pay rent in a new place. So we moved back into the forest—again. That was October of 2010.

Our family lived in tents four times between 2008 and 2013, and looking back I see it all as a gift. The time we spent living in the woods with the bare necessities, with the support and love of our family and friends, is what has taught me to be unmessable. It proved to me that what is most important in this world is not the stuff we have, but the people we love and the people who love us. I learned about patience, determination, resilience, and faith. Faith, in particular, truly filled the void in my life. I thank God for Brent and his initiative to do something unconventional. Otherwise, we wouldn't have had all these opportunities to learn and grow. If the financial crisis hadn't happened and we had stayed at Main Street, I don't believe we would have become the same close family we are today. These experiences showed our children what it takes to get through tough times and instilled in us all new perspectives. Our kids are amazing people, filled with compassion, understanding, and maturity that only a challenge like ours could bring about in people so young.

Jade on The Ellen DeGeneres Show, 2015

The next five years brought about seven more moves in three states, including one stint living with Brent's sister, Kari, for six months, as Jade was now in college and Kari and her husband, Tim, had moved to Florida with enough room to house our crew while we figured out our next moves. After Florida, the four of us lived in an extended-stay hotel for six months in Austin, Texas. We were working our way out of the financial hole we had dug for ourselves. Bankruptcy ruined our credit, and we still had some personal debts that were not forgiven in the process. We continued to scope out a way to use our construction knowledge to pay the bills while we kept eyes on our goal to get back into the construction business.

In 2015 Jade, by that time 21, wrote an email to *The Ellen DeGeneres Show* describing our adventure and how we had learned that even though we may have lost everything, we not only survived but also thrived because we had one another, and we chose a new perspective. The producer invited Jade and me to Burbank to see the show, and Ellen surprised us by inviting Jade on stage to read the letter she sent to the show and then presented us a check from Shutterfly for $20,000.

This gesture was real proof and validated that what we had been through was tough, but through the ups and downs, we had done a fantastic job of not only keeping our family together and making the best of a challenging situation, but we had managed to thrive in the midst of chaos. The money helped to buy some tools to get us back into the construction business and buy some nonessential items that we had put off purchasing for many years, such as cable TV and new clothes.

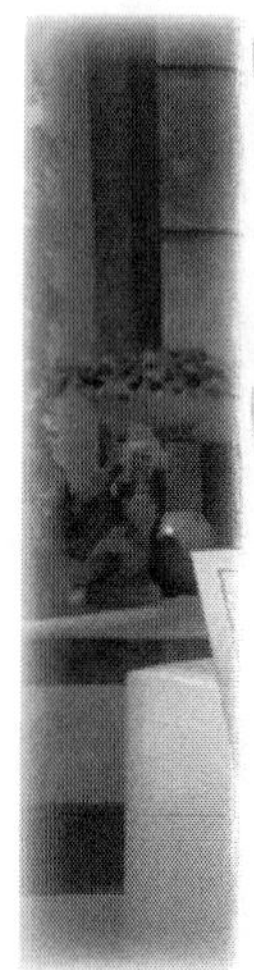

Shutterfly check presented to The Pohlman Family on The Ellen DeGeneres Show, 2015 (Photo by YouTube.com/TheEllenShow)

We embark on many adventures in our lifetime; making plans and sketching out ideas of what we aim to create. One thing I've learned is that change is inevitable and often happens when you least expect it. It can cause us great suffering and can also be a gift.

By mid 2020 we had just been through months of the COVID-19 crisis. Up to that point, the year had been one of rebirth for us both. The pandemic, although difficult and damaging to many, gave me the extra push to finish this book, Bren[illegible] and I closed on our first property purchase since 2008, and our construction business signed our largest-ever renovation contract. We paid cash for ten acres in New Mexico and drew up plans to build ourselves a small three-bedroom house overlooking the Pecos River, with views of beautiful mountains in the distance. September of 2020 was the first time in our thirty years together we had ever lived without a rent or mortgage payment—without being homeless.

We can all be unmessable and handle unexpected challenges that life throws our way. We can not only survive, getting back up from the knockdowns more quickly, strongly, and gracefully, but also with the ability to thrive under any circumstance. We can learn to become unmessable.

I have traveled quite a winding road to get to this point, and I wouldn't change a thing. The lessons learned are priceless, and the character it has built in me is boundless. I know there is nothing I cannot take on. I am strong. I am unmessable.

My story is not rare, especially in 2020. Because of the economic turmoil brought about by this pandemic, countless families will be in dire straits, and I am sure some, like us, will be living in tents. But, also like us, they can get through it if they can tap into their inner strength and resources to find the resilience that is within them. I was blessed to be able to find what life was teaching me and how to share my process with you. You see, there are times in everyone's life that being unmessable is the key to not only getting through it but also receiving the gift of it. And it doesn't matter if you're in what seems like a precarious situation caused by your own actions or an event over which you have had no control—you still need to find what it takes to go on, to move forward one step at a time. And while you're there, you might as well find out what life is trying to tell you.

Chapter 4

BEING UNMESSABLE

BY NOW YOU PROBABLY HAVE A GOOD IDEA of what it means to be unmessable, but just to make sure, being unmessable, in my opinion, is about who you choose to be in the face of those stressful circumstances—health challenges, criticism, divorce, financial crisis. It's about being resilient, not perfect. Life *is* going to throw curve balls at you. It's a given. We've all experienced it. We make a great plan, think of every detail, and then, poof, it changes. Just because life throws you to the mat doesn't mean that you have to tap out. Being unmessable is about having the ability to create possibilities when it seems like there are none and to get up more quickly, with less suffering and less recovery time, no matter what life hands you. It means being able to hear what other people say to you without getting high blood pressure. It means staying calm and steady, even when your world is falling apart, all the while being true to your beautiful, precious self.

We all need to face challenges in life and deal with people who sometimes try to knock us down or hurt us. We are all human.

But what if you could face them or the critics on social media with a bright, beautiful smile, navigate the calamities and crises at your job or business with steadiness and strength, and steer through the challenging twists and triggers of relationships with compassion and understanding?

Imagine what if you were able to do these things with that level of resilience, what you could accomplish.

Think of being unmessable as being one of those little Hasbro Playskool Weebles that were popular back in the '70s and had this catchphrase: "Weebles wobble, but they don't fall down."

Being unmessable means not letting things that knock you down keep you down. Practicing the strategies I've outlined in this book, you will get back up on your feet faster, be stronger with less of an emotional hangover, and be able to move forward to a life with new possibilities.

This book will show you the how, but it's up to you to practice and commit to what it takes to be unmessable in your own life. I want this for everyone, especially women! If I can access this level of resilience within myself, you can too!

My intention is that you will learn from my experiences without having to go through them yourself. If you do go through something similar, you'll then have an awareness that you wouldn't have had otherwise, an awareness that will allow you to make the choices that will keep you on the path to being true to yourself while striving to get what you *really* want most in this life.

Being unmessable doesn't mean you'll avoid suffering altogether, but it does mean you'll be able to develop the ability to minimize it, enjoy the journey more, and move forward faster.

Chapter 5

LIFE IS SHORT. GETTING THE MOST FROM THIS BOOK

BEFORE YOU CONTINUE READING, I urge you to create a space in your daily life to devote to learning the skills needed for becoming unmessable. First, think about the best way for you to absorb information. Maybe you absorb information sitting upright at your desk in a resourceful state, and maybe you need to find a quiet reading space that is comfortable. What kind of space works best for you? Maybe it's a certain time of day that works best. Are there objects you need to have in your space that help anchor you, help you feel in alignment with the steps needed to achieve your new way of being? Do you need to let your family know that for the next hour you are in a meeting with yourself? Consider what will best support you for this learning.

For me, the fragrances of lavender essential oil and cherry blossom incense put my brain in a very open state and anchor me in a way that keeps me alert, creative, and thoughtful. Keeping a journal is also integral to this process, and you may enjoy using colored pens or doodling pictures while you're reading this book in order to help you remember certain points that I will make. Or you may journal in the traditional way and simply write whatever comes to mind. Either way, you will need a journal to record answers to the chapter questions since your answers will enable you to personalize the process at the end of the book. It's entirely up to you how you do this. This is all about you.

Each chapter in this book is designed to help you create a personalized process that will lead you to becoming unmessable when facing any challenge. Each chapter ends with questions to ask yourself or exercises to do. Please take the time and space needed to ponder each question and write down in your journal the answers as well as any thoughts you have while doing the exercises. Don't be surprised to see patterns and themes in your thinking and behavior throughout your notes. That will be helpful for your growth.

Be sure to join our amazing community on Facebook called Be Unmessable Community.

And for real growth and integration of these principals, join our Be Unmessable Book Study on https://tinyurl.com/beunmessablebookstudy.

The following chapters comprise my process to becoming unmessable. Enjoy the journey!

Part II

LIVE ANOTHER WAY

Chapter 6

ANOTHER WAY TO SEE

BEING ABLE TO SEE ANOTHER WAY is an essential component and the first step toward becoming unmessable and getting what you *really* want in life. By the end of this chapter, you will have both an understanding of how to form your vision for the life you want and a new perspective on how to focus on achieving it.

To begin, you first need to think about what you want in this short life. I mean *really* want. If you don't know yet, it's because you probably haven't intentionally explored or focused on your deepest wishes. The best way to achieve your deepest wishes is to tap into that burning desire smoldering inside of you, that thing you keep putting off or trying to ignore. We all have at least one, so zero in on yours. Really focus on it. The object is to try to see it as it will be when you achieve it.

VISION AND FOCUS

Once you identify what you really want to achieve, your mind will start searching for the necessary people, opportunities, and support to achieve it. Identify this vision—or if you prefer, you can also call it your goal or destination—and your brain will automatically kick in and get to work helping you reach it.

There are many familiar sayings that come to mind when describing how to utilize the concept of focus and vision, and you probably already know them. So choose the ones that will best assist you on your journey.

- Keep your eye on the prize.
- Where focus goes, energy flows.
- If you don't know what you want, you're probably not going to get it.

Be Your Own Personal Success Coach

Before continuing on with this chapter, I want you to take some time to think about your life from the perspective of a personal success coach since you know yourself better than anyone. You are privy to all the little things you say to yourself, all the good and all the bad. You also hear the requests you are not asking for out loud, which include the dreams you are putting off and the deepest desires of your heart.

A personal success coach would ask you to reflect on the following questions: What have you heard while you've been eavesdropping on yourself? What do you really want most? What have you been delaying or making excuses about? What are you not asking for? What burning desires come up over and over and over again? Take your time and give these questions an opportunity to percolate. When you feel prepared to answer them, pull out your journal and at the same time jump to the For Your Journal section of this chapter and follow the Guided Visualization instructions. Then come back to this spot when you are finished.

You should now have one or two thoughts that came to you from the messenger you visualized in the guided visualization. You can use these thoughts and ideas as an initial vision while you continue to explore having a vision and seeing in a new way.

Know Where You Are Headed

Author and physician Deepak Chopra and Harvard Medical School professor Rudolph Tanzi in their 2012 book *Super Brain* suggest that when people become self-aware and intentional, they are actually teaching their brains to move much further than they are currently able. They describe how our brain is always listening to our thoughts and that we can teach our brain either to be limited or unlimited. But before you can make that leap, you need to know where you're going before you can educate your brain so that it can get you there. When you want to hit a target, it's helpful to know where the target is.

Of course, the plans we make in this life don't always turn out the way we think they will, but with a targeted vision, you plot a course that you can always get back on when life takes you in an unexpected direction. You may not be aware of this fact, but when a wind gust or other weather conditions throw a plane's angle off, it has the ability to self-correct when in autopilot to remain on course. The GPS always has a clear, definite vision of the destination programmed into it, like you are now doing in your life. For example, perhaps the destination is O'Hare airport in Chicago. The plan was to fly by way of the northern route, but unexpected weather changes dictated an easier and safer way by the southern route. Make sense? An adjustment and change *is* needed, but the destination remains constant.

It's the same in life. After living in the forest for a couple of weeks, I was feeling pretty low. The honeymoon phase of watching the kids play excitedly in the woods was wearing off, and reality intruded. I still didn't have a job, and neither of us had income. We were chewing through the little money we had, and the kids were slowly becoming restless and disenchanted. I was feeling hopeless. My internal talk was saying things like this: "Are we ever going to get out of here? I can't believe this is happening to us. I just want to go home and sit on a couch."

That was because I couldn't see any way out and was unable to focus on anything but our immediate situation and the feelings of uncertainty, sadness, and frustration that came with it. It was like our plane had veered off course into unknown territory. Life was different and uncertain, and trying to find schools for the children and jobs for us was difficult to do. It was easier for me to go to my hopeless place, my stick-my-head-in-the-sand-and-just-survive place. However, that changed when I slowed down my brain and discovered that our "plane" hadn't gone down. We were just experiencing turbulence, and eventually we would be back on course. You see—all our basic needs were being met. We had air, food, water, shelter, clothing, a place to sleep, and love of family. It wasn't exactly how we wanted to be living our life, but we had more than enough.

It was our situation and not our desires and hopes that had changed. Our vision to keep our family together and love one another, to teach our kids to be the best they could be, to strive for excellence, to be self-employed, and to fulfill becoming what we were created to be was still intact. The pursuit of that vision helped to spur our dream machine. We spent time driving around the local area looking at real estate and rental possibilities even though we didn't have the money to rent anything. We scouted out neighborhoods and inquired about enrollment in local charter schools although we didn't have an address yet. Brent and I got busy checking out local job opportunities for me and remembered a friend had told us about a guy who was moving to Flagstaff to head up a start-up company, the one I mentioned in chapter three. Our dream started to become real.

Like us, you must set your course, envision where you want to go, make a plan to get there, and embark on it. When detours—and I guarantee life will throw you detours—come up, go for the ride. Use this time to reassess the voyage and make any necessary course corrections and remain focused on your destination.

Never Give Up on a Dream Because of a Course Change

When you are trying to achieve something you really want in life but get thrown off course, stay focused, and never give up. You can always figure out how to get back on course if you trust yourself and let your brain sift through all the possible new, and sometimes even better, routes. Take some time and space to explore possibilities. Trust in yourself. The answer is there; you just need to create a new way to allow it to form and surface.

PROGRAM YOUR VISION (DESTINATION/GOAL)

To begin, determine what your vision (destination/goal) should include, such as these examples:

- an intimate relationship that is fun, passionate, respectful, and loving
- a healthy body so you have energy to enjoy your family for the long term
- a deeply satisfying job or business that excites you and challenges you
- (add your own) ____________________

Remember that staying focused on your vision (destination/goal) is keeping you moving in the correct direction and that you must always remain flexible on *how you get there.*

When Life Throws Detours

When life throws you detours in the form of challenges, struggles, and pain, your vision is what gives you the momentum to move forward. Focus on your vision.

Life certainly threw us detours. Life seemed on track after we moved into the house on Harmony Lane and the kids began school, and we planned how and when we would get our belongings back. Then we experienced yet another detour. Amethyst became ill. She began throwing up, and her brother and sister also began feeling sick. Then the clincher: Brent started feeling ill.

All had stu noses and were unable to breathe properly. The kids felt good enough to g to school during the day, but they felt sick when they got home. Brent suspe ed mold. He and I hunted for it all through the house and came across a hid n attic room above Amethyst's bedroom loft. When we opened the door, th e it was—mold!

This de ur was definitely unexpected and one we didn't want or expect or like. Sinc he owners weren't planning on fixing it anytime soon, Brent was adamant th we needed to move ASAP. Back into the national forest we went for a few m e weeks. But once there, we immediately resumed our hunt for another ho e. We kept our vision real and in focus.

Anytim you want or need to change or shift- anything in life—be it your job, relation ip, health, or living location—the road to that change starts first by being ab to *see* it as your future.

Conscious a Unconscious Visions

We all h e conscious visions as well as unconscious ones. The unconscious ones are th most of us aren't aware we've been harboring. This unconscious vision coul e as simple as wanting to keep your life as it is. Therefore, we don't really nsider it a vision. I'm betting that if you cannot come up with your curren ision, it's possible that—at least in some areas of your life—your vision may to maintain the status quo so that there are no surprises and you can fee afe and secure. But your vision, be it conscious or unconscious, is still your ion. Even if it is one you didn't consciously choose, your brain is program d to gravitate toward achieving it. Life is short, and if you want to be unme able, my advice is to take an active approach toward achieving any vision y may have.

Unmasking nconscious Visions

In orde o proactively discover any unconscious visions so you can intentionally poi them in the path you really want to travel, I suggest you hire a personal success coach if you find you can't do it on your own. While I was working with one particular client, Jen, I noticed that she was trying to please her mom all the time even though she didn't realize it. In this case, her unconscious vision was to make her mom always feel great so that she, in turn, would feel accepted and loved. Once she discovered that so much of her time and effort was spent trying to achieve this fruitless vision, she was able to make changes that gave her loads more energy as she changed her focus to her daughter and her new husband and their new son. She became unmessable.

Start Today!

In order to get what you *really* want in life, you need to let go of whatever baggage you are lugging around that you can't let go of. Kim Standeven, founder of Draw in the Magic, a company that helps people tune out the distractions of life by accessing their energetic wisdom, has this advice: Pretend you are holding a glass of water that represents your life or situation. If you want to experience something new, you cannot do so unless you let go of the glass. You could pick up another object and still continue to hold onto the glass, but you will never fully experience the new object until you put down that glass and stop concerning yourself with it. This is the same with your vision. If you continue to hold onto a vision that is leading you away from what you really want most, you will never be able to fully experience the new vision. You must let go of the old. You can have more than one vision for your life but cannot simultaneously move toward achieving two or more visions that oppose one another. That is why you need to identify any unconscious visions that may be holding you back from achieving what you really want most.

I'm a perfect example of this. Brent and I held onto Main Street until it was a nonviable option. We chewed through our savings and the equity in the house to keep it. We hung on by our fingertips till it was super painful. Only when we finally accepted that we needed to let go of the house and let the lender foreclose and also to let go of the business and file for bankruptcy were we able to e ›erience and pursue something new!

Maybe s also time for you to let go of what is holding you back from pursuing so ething new. Chances are, the reason you aren't moving forward toward ach ring the vision you have or the reason you resisted making the changes nee ed to step into that vision isn't the same as those shabby reasons you always me up with. Chances are it's because the real reason is so simple that you coı tantly overlook it. It's not the obvious obstacles we trip over; it's the ones we on't see that trip us up! Think of a vision you gave up on because life threw a tour your way. I'm not talking about the visions that you decided were not be for you. I'm talking about the ones that you really wanted but gave up on. bet that once you look deeper, take some time to think of possibilities, you an see a way to make it happen. Maybe it involved letting go of something, aybe a belief or maybe a person. It's the things we don't see that trip us up, s ake some time to reflect and see all the possibilities.

A visioı s an intentional destination, your main target. It is the initial step you must ta to become unmessable. Once you know what you really want, it's much ea er to let go of the things that no longer serve you and easier to focus on th hings that allow you to more easily attain your vision.

PERSPEC IVE

Seeing other way and living your life in a different way than it is means changing yc r perspective. Try taking a different view or vantage point, or explore new ossibilities when things go awry or don't make sense. By choosing to see life tł ugh various lenses, you are opening up to seeing what exists in your life anı ıow these things influence the direction your life is taking. With a new persp tive, you'll be able to look at these things differently and see how your world ill change and shift when your perspective is either modified or ditched con letely. Compare what you find and then choose what you want. Albert Eins in is believed to have said, "We can't solve problems by using the same kind c thinking we used when we created them."

When we get locked into only one way of seeing, be it our view of a situation, a person, or even ourselves, it limits us. So, in being open to the way you see and being willing to change your perspective, you can intentionally and consciously choose what to focus on and with which lens to view your future to achieve the vision you actually desire.

For example, have you ever put on someone's glasses, and when you tried to look through the lenses, you were caught by surprise? Maybe what you saw was blurry and distorted, or maybe it was super clear and bright. If these were sunglasses, maybe you were even able to view nature in a new hue, a new way. Seeing anything through a different lens is exactly what we need to help us shift and grow.

I found this out when we arrived at that first campsite in Parks, Arizona. I was tentative. I was completely out of my element. I wasn't sure what to expect; would there be wild animals, random backpackers, or complete silence? I had no idea. But my mama instinct alerted me to be careful. In this situation, my lens was security; I had to keep my family safe and secure. Brent, on the other hand, was all about adventure! He wanted to clear the area and set up our campsite so we could all head out on our first hike and explore the unknown territory.

The kids didn't seem scared at all. They were looking through their dad's eyes and exploring their new temporary home. They played with pinecones and sticks and climbed on boulders and played hide-and-go-seek. It was just another playday for them, different location. Fear or security was not in their vision; their lens was on playing.

Each of us makes a decision when it comes to what we want or need to focus on in life. Some of us focus on everything that is going wrong whereas others focus on all that is right and wonderful. That's not to say we only have those two choices. In life there are endless possibilities. The important thing is that whatever you choose to focus on is what your brain is going to work toward. This means if you choose to focus on the problem at hand, whatever it is, that pr blem will grow in your mind. But when you choose to focus on a *solution* t hat problem and on the path that leads toward your vision, it will grow in what you desire. Humans have been wrestling with this choice for millenn

> *One eve ng an old Cherokee man told his grandson about a battle that goe n inside people.*
>
> *He said My son, the battle is between two 'wolves' inside us all. One is evil. s anger, envy, jealousy, sorrow, regret, greed, arrogance, self-pity, gu , resentment, inferiority, lies, false pride, superiority, and ego*
>
> *The oth is good. It is joy, peace, love, hope, serenity, humility, kindness, be volence, empathy, generosity, truth, compassion, and faith."*
>
> *The gra lson thought about it for a minute and then asked his grandfa er,*
>
> *"Which olf wins?"*
>
> *The old herokee man replied, "The one you feed."*

You see vhen we choose to keep our focus on what is challenging in our life—focus eas such as the dog peeing in the house, not making enough money, shor alls in a husband's romanticism, or employees calling in sick—life becomes a c llenge. The stress and frustration builds up. We become consumed with the fe ngs of suffering that are connected to those problems and the negative em ions that go along with them. This type of focus will never lead you to your imate vision. To shift out of this, you need to intentionally choose what you focus on, something that aligns with your vision and gets you to where you want to be. If your vision is to have a loving relationship filled with joy and passion, then focusing on how your partner doesn't measure up is never going to get you there. Think about it. If you want love, joy, and passion, then focus on those and influence your internal conversation to say words that convey those feelings and that work toward achieving that type of relationship.

Refocusing

This means that your perspective needs to be continually refocused to keep your vision clear and within your sight. Once you practice being mindful enough and become skillful at noticing your internal conversation (what you say to yourself and what you focus on most of the time), you will then be able to pause and make the necessary changes and adjustments in your perspective that play an incredibly important part in becoming unmessable.

The move to the national forest brought me a deep sense of shame and a feeling that I had let my kids down. My focus was on that and, by extension, how that made me a bad person. This focus influenced the direction my life was going, and it wasn't getting any better.

Every interaction with the kids and my husband went through that lens of shame and disappointment in my head. That led me to scrutinize my interactions with the kids. If I thought they were mad at me, I asked myself whether I should make a big deal about their misbehavior or whether I should let that misbehavior go so that they wouldn't hold a grudge against me. I focused through that lens until everything was seen as building a case that I was a bad mom. Brent didn't have this problem. When I shared with him my feelings of failure, he said, "Oh, I wouldn't even worry about that!" He obviously had a different perspective. He looked for the fun, the adventure, and the challenge. Seeing that in him made me change my perspective. As this new perspective slowly evolved, I saw new possibilities. The kids were becoming resilient, learning how to keep going even when it was tough, how to never give up, and how to love ne another even when they didn't agree.

You car lso use other people's perspectives to learn how to get what you want. Is the someone you know or know of who has what you want? Is there someone el you admire who is living life the way you would like to? Try to break dowr ıow they made that happen. What is their focus, what lens do they see the life through, and what is their ultimate vision? Answering these questions c help you learn how the people who are successfully living the way you wa to be living reached that place.

Choosing Yo Lens

As I di ɔvered, in order to be unmessable you need to be intentional about what ns you choose to look through. When you own your power, you have influer e over your life events, and that in turn allows you to experience far less suff ing, frustration, annoyance, and shame. This is what happens when you c ɔose your best lens.

Pick a l s that allows you to do the following:

- Fo s on the good!
- Fo s on the abundance!
- Fo s on the radiance and the glitter!
- Fo s on the world you want!
- Fo s on things you never saw before!

You alw ys have the ability to be unmessable and to choose your focus no matter the c cumstance.

FOR YOUR JOURNAL

Life Wheel

The Life Wheel is something I was introduced to years ago by several other success coaches who utilized this tool. The Life Wheel works because it enables you to segment and then rate the various areas of your life. Doing this allows you to take a closer look at what's going on in your life and then prioritize where you want to do some refocusing. I have found this to be very helpful since it has shown me where I am most satisfied and most dissatisfied and where I need to work on refocusing. Ideally, you should feel free to come back to this exercise at any time both to confirm where you have improved and to define new areas to work on and old ones that still need attention. Now get what you need to start working in your journal.

1. Draw a Life Wheel circle, like the example below, in your journal.

2. Fill in the top portion of each section on the life wheel with names for the areas of your life you want to examine more closely. For example, the areas might include career, health, time, marriage or relationship, friends, hobbies, self-care, parenting, job, business, spirituality, family, financial, education, etc. Pick the ones that work best for you.

3. Next, in the inner portion of each section of the life wheel, rate each area with a number from one to ten, with one meaning completely dissatisfied with how unmessable you are in this area and ten meaning completely satisfied with how unmessable you are in this area.

Example:

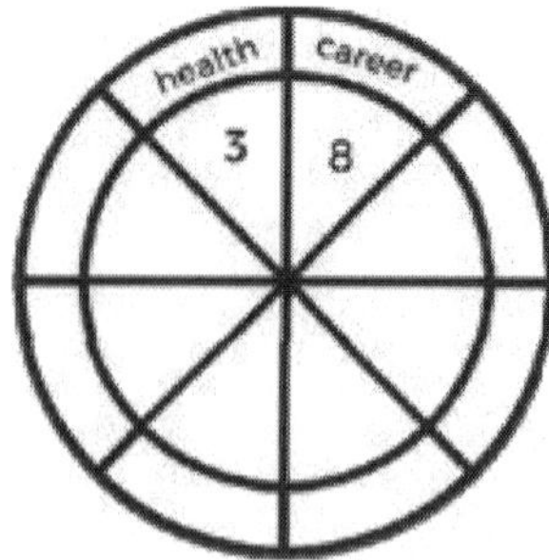

4. In your journal, answer each of the following questions in as much detail as you need. This exercise is meant to help you rediscover things in your life that you have taken for granted or overlooked or didn't think of as important.

    a. Can you describe the reasoning for scoring each area as you did?

    b. Are you surprised by any of the reasons you gave?

    c. Is there a pattern or theme to your reasonings?

    d. What do you consider the top two areas on which you need to refocus your attention?

    e. For each of these two areas, what do you envision? What new things would you like to see?

When you are finished writing your entries, put them away for a day or two and then reread what you wrote. You might be surprised, or it may jog your memory or perception of what is truly important in your life. Revise any necessary entries as you see fit. Once you do this, you can proceed to the Fine

Tune Your Perspective exercise, or you may choose to again go through the guided visualization that follows.

Guided Visualization

Life can get so busy sometimes that we don't take the time or create the space to listen to what our inner guidance is trying to tell us. In this chapter I talked about how people ignore their inner desires. This visualization is designed to help you tap into your intuition, your inner guide, God, the universe, or whatever else you might call that source of guidance and hear what that guidance is telling you. This will help you to create a compelling vision for your life. You can use this visualization again and again to help you listen to your inner messenger. You can complete this comfortably in about ten minutes, or you can take longer if you wish. It's up to you. I suggest that you keep your journal nearby so you can jot down any thoughts or prompts you may encounter. These notes are great to go back to later and again see if there are any themes or patterns.

The guided visualization is written out below, and if you prefer to listen along, rather than reading, an audio version can be found at karenpohlman.com/guided-visualization.

- Find a quiet place to perform the visualization.
- Sit in a comfortable seat with your arms and legs relaxed.
- Take several deep breaths in through your nose and let them out easily through your mouth.
- Let go of any thoughts that are not allowing you to be in this exact place at this time.
- Picture there is a beautiful glistening beam of light that is coming down from the heavens down into your body. You are connected to the divine energy of your creator.
- Then picture there is a root system like a tree coming down from you deep into the core of the earth. You are grounded.

- Take another deep breath and let it out
- Think of a time when you were truly grateful; let yourself enjoy the gratitude. Think of a time when you were truly proud of yourself; enjoy the moment and feel the joy. Think of a time when you felt so cared for; enjoy that moment and feel the love. You are safe, you are grounded, you are loved, and you are valuable.
- From this safe place, you can see a glistening messenger walking toward you. This messenger is here to guide you for your highest and best good.
- Ask this messenger, "What message do you have for me?"
- Then ask, "For my highest and best good, where should I be focused?"
- Notice anything around you—objects, pictures, words—and take note of all you see, hear, or experience.
- Thank the messenger for any messages given to you.
- Breathe in and breathe out. Slowly open your eyes.

Take out your journal and do the following:

- Write down any thoughts that surfaced during your guided visualization. There is no need to edit these thoughts; they can be anything!
- Take some time to think of any themes that emerged.
- Did you find any surprises or have any epiphanies?
- Were your two main areas of focus the same after the visualization exercise? If they changed, that's OK. Now is the time to focus on where your heart and intuition are guiding you.
- Summarize your vision for your two areas of focus.
- Consider what you need to let go of in order to have new experiences in those areas. List them.

Fine Tune Your Perspective: An Exercise

Recall a story that has been with you throughout your life. We all have at least one that is always with us that we tap into now and again. You know; it's the one you regularly repeat to yourself that cements your thoughts or justification about something. Write down a few sentences that describe that event or story. After you feel like the story is complete, choose a new lens with which to view this story. Pick one of the following lenses and rewrite your story through this new lens: lens of the other person, lens of learning, lens of gratitude. You don't have to keep this story after you are done, but the act of writing the story from a different perspective will enable you to see things you didn't see before. When you are done with this exercise, write down what you learned in your journal.

CHAPTER TAKEAWAYS

1. Create a vision for your life and write about it in detail in your journal. Read it often to keep the vision alive.

2. Remember if you don't create a vision, you will instead be following an unconscious one that you do not control and may lead you where you don't want to go.

3. When life gets turbulent, hang in there, correct course, and stay focused on your vision.

4. Be open to changing perspective; life changes, and so can you.

5. Perspective is the lens you use to focus on your vision. Choose it carefully and refocus and adjust when needed.

Chapter 7

ANOTHER WAY TO THINK

THIS CHAPTER EXPLAINS HOW a certain type of our thinking holds us in autopilot, drives behaviors, and stops us from revealing our true selves. Changing this type of thinking leads to being unmessable and getting what you really want most out of life.

AUTOPILOT

Being on autopilot means fixating on a biased way of seeing ourselves, other people, and the world. Think about it. There might be a familiar story you often tell yourself about a certain family member, friend, or event, and if it always surfaces when you see a certain person, you're on autopilot. This familiar story enables that voice in your head to repeat the same old details embedded in your brain as you automatically experience the same visual and auditory reactions you've had before based on your own version of what really took place and sometimes not the way others remember the same person or event.

Changing this automatic recall is essential for freeing up the ability to rethink events and people in our lives and change perspective that, in turn, helps us to get unstuck and be able to objectively examine the past in order to create an unmessable life.

Let me tell you why we get stuck in autopilot. You're not crazy. I promise!

How Autopilot Works

"The brain is literally the most complex object in the known universe," Christof Koch, chief scientific officer of the Allen Institute for Brain Science, told NPR in 2013. It's always "on," with billions of neurons firing continuously to keep your body functioning. As our hearts beat and lungs breathe, physically we are essentially on autopilot.

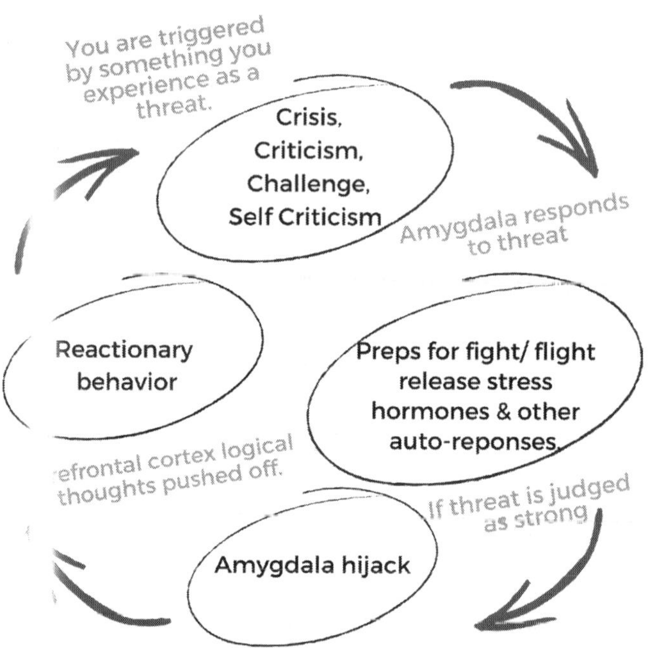

Your body produces a variety of neurochemicals such as adrenaline, cortisol, dopamine, and serotonin to assist the cells in the nervous system in "talking" to one another. The number of neurochemicals produced fluctuates, depending on individual needs and coordinate nervous system responses. Working together, these chemical "cocktails" help to produce physical effects in life experiences, behaviors, and relationships. These physical expressions include heart pounding, deeply relaxed muscles, high or low voice pitches and tones, changes in dilation of the eyes, and skin effects such as goose bumps.

Most brain activity is unconscious, automatic, superfast, and forever outside our awareness. Then there is a slower action we call "thought," which we can observe, study, and change.

From the moment of birth—and some scientists even claim the starting point is in utero—to the present, every event and experience in our lives has influenced our brain and our thinking. We humans share much genetically, but our individual experiences, which the brain stores as memories, are what *really* make each of us unique. We each have unique life experiences.

These memories are stored by the brain, which then references them with various neurochemical "cocktails" that form our beliefs and help us make the decisions and choices to ensure our survival. The brain is designed to access this information and use it to create a program that it uses on autopilot to make quick and efficient decisions, conserving energy. This process is what develops our beliefs about events, people, and the world, and that can either work to our advantage or detriment.

In Don Miguel Ruiz's 1997 book, *The Four Agreements*, this programming is referred to as domestication, and he says it's the operating system from childhood that teaches us how to be human. The beliefs of our parents, teachers, religious leaders, employers, friends, neighbors, and relatives—combined with the influence of television, music, movies, etc.—essentially teach us how to do life by rewarding good behavior and punishing bad behavior. This learned programming puts our decisions on autopilot.

The Mind

The mind makes both subconscious and conscious interpretations and assumptions using the information the brain stores from life events you experience. The subconscious mind is set up to protect you by allowing you to make survival decisions quickly on autopilot.

On the other hand, the conscious mind can also disengage and separate itself from autopilot mode and respond to make intentional, deliberate, and purposeful decisions, like the pilot seated in a plane. This separation, however, is what takes self-awareness, focus, and practice to accomplish.

The incredible mind is also capable of causing substantial changes in the physical brain. For example, scientists have shown that intentional thoughts of gratitude can trigger physical circuits in the brain that minimize the release of the neurochemical stress hormones cortisol and adrenaline while increasing the feel-good ones oxytocin and dopamine. These thoughts of gratitude actually change the brain by reinforcing the pathways through which these thoughts travel, so the pathways become thicker and stronger, allowing us an easier return to that pathway whenever needed. While living in the national forest, one of our family rituals was what we called "gratefuls." We did this when the kids began fighting in the car, or I was emotionally shutting down, or Brent was exasperated trying to solve problems. One of us would call out the request for five gratefuls each, a total of twenty-five, and a request for who was going to start. Each of us would take turns calling out one thing we were grateful for. These were often simple things such as sunny skies, healthy bodies, the ability to chat with family, or having the gasoline needed to get us where we were going.

Calling out our gratefuls changed our brain chemistry, and our attitudes improved in an instant. This thinking usually encouraged positive conversation and connection, with a lighter and funnier tone to pause and reset the temporary breakdown. This reset gave us the chance to refocus attention and vision on what was good in our lives since it made us focus on sufficiency rather than loss. We took control of thoughts to become unmessable during a detour in life.

It's really easy for anyone to fall into autopilot when things aren't going well. We're tired, stressed, and feeling out of control, and our brains get hijacked by the chemicals released when we feel attacked by life.

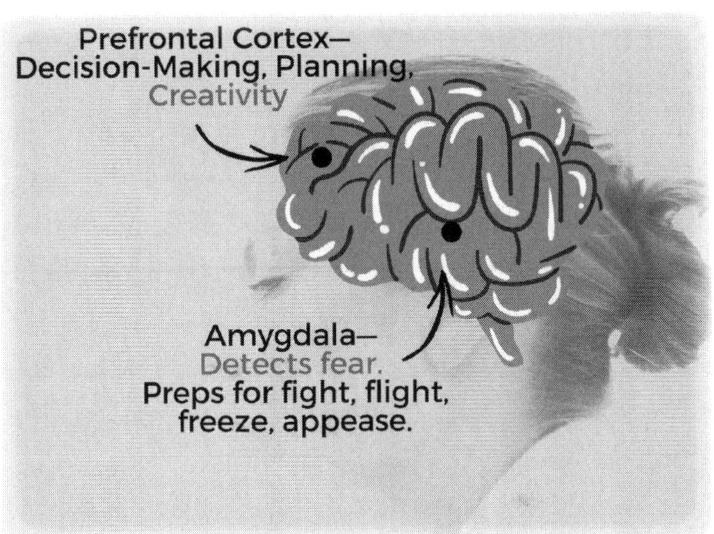

Triggers

When a thought or event triggers something that your brain experiences as a threat, it switches to autopilot mode. This could be an actual physical threat, but often it is brought on by a criticism or judgment from another person or even a loud voice or a loud noise. When the brain processes these threats, the limbic system, where all of your old memories are stored, is activated. Part of this limbic system, the amygdala, goes into overdrive and triggers the release of cortisol and adrenaline, which in turn triggers a fight-or-flight, freeze-or-appease response. This is when the heart beats faster, blood pressure rises, and body temperature rises or falls.

Sergio Della Sala, a cognitive neuroscientist at the University of Edinburgh in Scotland, explains that the brain works with irrational assumptions in its attempt to keep you safe and alive. In addition, Rick Hanson, PhD, in his paper

"Your Wonderful Brain," says that the brain creates views and beliefs about the state of the world, the body, and the mind, and we need to understand that these views and beliefs are "best-guess, probably-at-least-partly-wrong, and always incomplete formulations about reality." So, when you are completely convinced that you are absolutely right about an event or story or person, chances are your brain has constructed a distorted view, and you may be partially incorrect.

Because the brain is adept at creating shortcuts designed to keep us energized and safe, it sometimes creates false memories, if that is what it takes. Della Sala's research also concluded that the brain's quick decision-making based on survival mode creates false memories that are the byproduct of a memory system that works well and is also a sign of a healthy brain. I know it seems hard to believe that the memory system is working well when it creates false memories, but many of our everyday memories are falsely reconstructed because our unique view of the world is continually changing. What this boils down to is that it is mostly guesswork! The brain reads between the lines, making assumptions to save time and to protect the human that it serves—you. It's doing you a favor! And it is done unconsciously. Our brains make up stories to help us get through life. We do it all the time, such as when we think we know what other people are thinking. We make up a story about what we believe is going on in their heads, why they do what they do, or what their intentions were prior to certain actions. When Brent and I went to counseling, I found out that many of the times I thought he was angry, he was actually just being silent and thinking about what I had said.

This unconscious reality is an autopilot program based on a bunch of best guesses that you believe are facts. This is human nature; we all do it. In fact, it's what we base most life decisions on. Unfortunately, this autopilot thinking is what holds us back from being unmessable and getting what we really want.

In my case, the fertile ground of financial crisis gave me and my family many opportunities to experience the responses of a hijacked brain and veer into autopilot. One night, flashing lights appeared in the driveway at Main Street, followed by a man knocking on the front door asking to repossess our car. After I requested a bit of time to gather my belongings, I quickly grabbed a black garbage bag and collected my things from inside the vehicle. The repo guy and Brent stood beside the car. In my head, I was scattered with disbelief and embarrassment. My body flooded with neurochemicals! I felt hot and sweaty. The reasoning part of my brain couldn't think creatively or strategically. Plus, it was making assumptions and drawing conclusions about the experience and about me, based on my previous beliefs, all at the same time. My amygdala was hijacked.

From the fight or flight choices, we appeased. The repossession company was taking our car away forever because we couldn't make the payments. Because my brain wasn't working at its best in that situation, I couldn't make wise decisions. In hindsight, for example, we should have taken the license plate off the car so the repo guy couldn't drive it. This is a perfect example of how the limbic system's fight/flight mode took over my brain. Months later we realized that Mr. Repo man drove our car another few thousand miles before turning it in, so we owed even more money due to the mileage he added.

Disengaging the Autopilot

When you need to spread your wings and get more out of life and can't seem to figure out why you are stuck, it's often because your brain is working on its autopilot program to keep you safe. This is through no fault of your own, but it is something you can change once you learn how to work the system.

When your amygdala is hijacked and not thinking creatively, it doesn't mean you can't override and disengage this autopilot program and make life changes. All it takes is self-awareness, refocus, and practice. Take time to calm yourself with deep breathing, taking a walk, or whatever allows you to reconnect with yourself. Some people find connection with creating through music, writing, dance, or art. Having a conscious mind and the ability to influence our brains to th k differently makes us extremely fortunate and blessed!

Challe e yourself to think about life's possibilities, as this releases your potential tc xperience massive amounts of joy, love, and abundance and get what you *r lly* want most! Whatever that is! And disengage the autopilot program as on as you can.

Fear

When e first arrived in the national forest, I shared with Brent my concern ab t bears and wolves, but Brent was way more concerned about humans tha animals. Our first night at the campsite sent me into autopilot fear mode. hen the sun went down, the noises of the night freaked me out. The loud, hi 1-pitched howling cries from multiple directions made me think that Cujo a the wolf pack had us surrounded. My brain was in autopilot fear spiral! Hija ed! Panic set in, and I convinced Brent to move the car closer to the tents in se I had to make a mad dash of heroic proportions to save the children wh n the wolf pack came to eat them.

Intentional inking

In orde o intentionally influence your brain to think differently, you need to harness t amazing capability of your mind and brain, try to take captive every thoug , and choose thoughts that align with your vision for your life.

Practic nonitoring your thoughts, and consciously choose whether or not to cont ue with the thoughts that arise. Use meditation and prayer to focus your oughts on things that align with your vision. This is how to set yourself up r success and how to have the best chance of getting what you want most i life, being unmessable and living a life that you absolutely love!

YOUR DF VING FORCE: CORE HUMAN NEEDS

To bec e unmessable, you need to figure out what drives your behavior so you c 1 change direction when needed. Robbins Madanes Training illuminates how humans are motivated by six core human needs which form their choices. Becoming aware of these needs made a huge difference in navigating my own life, which is why I am sharing them here.

The Six Human Needs

The first four of the six human needs are based on survival instinct and shape our personalities.

- Certainty
- Variety
- Significance
- Love/Connection

The final two human needs are spiritual and give life its purpose.

- Growth
- Contribution

Each of these drivers can cause you to choose behaviors that create positive, negative, and neutral results. It's up to you to choose intentionally, not unconsciously, the behaviors that will give you the best chance of reaching your vision for your life. When your thinking is on autopilot, you choose behaviors unconsciously that may meet your needs, but those behaviors don't always get you where you want to go. For example, we all need to feel safe, but if your need for safety leads you to hiding your true feelings, you may not get what you want in relationships.

On a daily basis, people focus on two of these needs more often than the remaining four. Notice which two needs you find yourself naturally gravitating toward, as reordering their importance later will enable you to shift what drives your autopilot mode and suffer less while experiencing more joy in your life.

Certainty

Feeling certain that you can avoid suffering and find comfort and joy in life is what makes you feel safe. When this certainty is at the top of your go-to needs, you probably prefer things to stay the same so you know what to expect. Certainty motivates us to try to control events and people or to hold onto familiar stories. Even when an old story takes you to a place of suffering in your head, the certainty you feel in knowing how the story plays out can radiate comfort. Making changes and shifts to create a new way of living creates some uncertainty, which may trigger you to hold onto old negative thoughts and memories as a type of security blanket. This will pass as you become more self-aware and continue to make new and better choices to fill your needs.

When we left Main Street, the uncertainty of our future caused me to lean into the old, familiar relationship patterns I shared with my husband. I couldn't feel secure enough to fill that need and was constantly anxious and unconsciously focused on controlling as much as I could. Trying to control things and people filled my need for certainty but made me not much fun to be around.

Variety

As much as we all need certainty, we also need variety, and we need to mix things up on a daily basis. Variety makes us feel great when we follow six months of working on the same project with a beach vacation or an incredible hiking trip. Variety can also lead some people to unconsciously start creating drama when unconsciously looking to make life interesting. Sure, we all need surprise, excitement, and new stimuli, but when variety is one of your top go-to needs, you may end up frequently changing jobs, relationships, or where you live just to feel the change.

Significance

People want to feel their lives matter and that they are important, unique, special, or needed. If significance is in your top go-to needs, you probably have a desire to be noticed, heard, and seen on a regular basis. This recognition can provide a sense of validation, a measurement to track significance, and it can take a variety of forms. Some people dye their hair a funky color or wear bold clothes, whereas others talk loudly or stir up conversations, longing to be noticed and relevant.

Looking back on Main Street, Brent and I often joke about what was a serious unconscious attempt at filling the need for significance. We built a house that covered 6,500 square feet, rose fifty feet and three stories high, and included a personal elevator, five-car garage, and guest house.

Love and Connection

Everyone wants to be loved. Love instills a sense of belonging and fosters relationships with one another. For those who don't feel loved, feeling connected is the next best thing. This is where social media exerts its strong pull because it allows a sense of connection with others. Those for whom love is a top go-to need often seek out close relationships with people and pets and participate in activities and go places where they feel connected. This drive can also take an unhealthy turn if it causes you to neglect yourself in order to care for others or to keep a toxic relationship going to feel connected.

Growth

Growth comes with learning and is a gift, an expansion of capability and understanding. Learning and trying new experiences are what help us grow, but if we start thinking we know it all, we stop growing. If your top go-to need is growth, you tend to strive to be better and keep learning throughout life. Switching jobs when you feel you've reached your full potential is good, but this top go-to need can also make you vulnerable to perfectionism and a lack of self-care.

Contribution

The contribution need is filled when helping, supporting, and giving to others. Choosing to incorporate this contribution need often fills many other primary needs as well. Think of when you've helped someone. You not only filled the need for contribution, but you probably also felt connected to that person or love for that person. Maybe you felt particularly significant because the person made a big deal about your generosity, and maybe the contribution added variety to your life because it was a change of pace from your regular routine. Contribution will most likely fill more than just the need to contribute. Contribution is where it's at when it comes to being unmessable! Keep in mind, though, that with contribution as a top go-to need, you may tend to forget about those closest to you. It can often be easier to give to those who don't know you very well. Remember to contribute to the people you are closest with and to whom you have given your heart. Incorporate this need as one of your top two needs consistently, and your need to hang onto destructive behaviors will effortlessly dissipate. Keeping focused on how you can contribute to the best in any situation will get you closer to being unmessable.

Take a look at the lowest-scoring two areas of the life wheel you constructed in chapter 6 and compare those areas with the needs on this list to identify why those areas may not be working well. What needs are you unconsciously focusing on in those areas? Knowing this information will permit you to choose alternative actions and behaviors that fill those needs and also get you to your vision.

Addictive Behavior and Why You Can't Just Stop

Today's addictions range from social media, food, television, gossiping, complaining, work, alcohol, being busy, drugs and even anger. Chances are, if you are filling three or more of your needs with one of these behaviors, it is addictive. Look back at the areas in your life that you identified in your life wheel that aren't working, and that will help you to determine which behaviors you have had difficulty stopping in the past. When a behavior is a struggle to quit, you are most likely using it to fill several needs simultaneously. So start by identifying those needs and make different choices in the behaviors you are using to fulfill them, replacing them with ones that not only fill your needs but also align better with your life vision.

Knowing what drives any behavior, especially destructive behavior, is helpful for choosing supportive alternatives that will ultimately lead you to the life you dream of living.

You can choose to fulfill these needs, consciously or unconsciously, with constructive and healthy behaviors, neutral behaviors, or destructive and unhealthy behaviors. It's up to you.

Once you determine what needs are driving you and then consciously choose constructive and healthy behavior, you empower your brain to lead you more quickly in the direction of being unmessable and where you want to be.

Do not conform to the pattern of this world, but be transformed by the renewing of your mind. ~Romans 12:2

When I coach women, I help them discover their top two needs and help them create new possibilities that also align with their vision. One of my clients, Janna, discovered one of her top two needs was certainty, which caused her to please people in an attempt to control her surroundings in order to feel less anxious. The work we did enabled her to put contribution and love above the certainty need which allowed her to make different choices and feel less anxious, without the people-pleasing drive. She became more comfortable being herself without guilt and felt more joy in her life. She is unmessable.

What Drives You?

- Certainty
- Variety
- Significance
- Love
- Growth
- Contribution

Make a Choice

Now you need to consciously choose which two human needs you are going to spend the most time filling with your behaviors and choices. Be conscious of which needs you are focusing on filling and intentionally choose the ones that will get you what you really want in life.

A word of caution: If you spend too much time choosing the illusion of certainty and significance, you will likely have recurring problems in your life. You could end up playing it safe, which would mean that the world would miss out on all of what only you can contribute. The pursuit of accolades, approval, and attention could cause you to miss out on lots of opportunities to connect and love.

Consciously choose the needs that drive your behaviors to align with your vision and get you where you want to go!

GUILT VERSUS SHAME

I could not leave this chapter without discussing another type of thinking that can often get in the way of reaching your vision. Just like human needs can drive your behaviors, when you confuse guilt and shame, it can throw you off course.

Guilt

Guilt is the uncomfortable feeling you get when you've missed the mark and have done something not in alignment with the type of person you want to be. Guilt propels a positive result, as it calls you to action, such as asking for forgiveness, making amends, and changing your behavior.

Shame

Shame, though related, is much different. When you miss the mark, make a mistake, or do something embarrassing, shame is a feeling that comes along and makes you feel small, flawed, and not good enough. It encompasses a fear of being unlovable and abandoned for your flaws. Humans are built for relationships, and when we feel that those connections could be severed—because shame leads us to believe our mistakes make us flawed or not good enough—we often hide from ourselves and one another.

When we lost our house and business and had to move, I felt a tremendous sense of shame. I didn't want anyone to know, thought we were the only ones going through this financial crisis, felt terrible about myself for our losses, and felt the shame continuing to grow inside as I kept it to myself.

Almost everyone experiences shame. One exception is a small percentage of people who don't experience any type of connection. Strong reactions such as rage, screaming, destruction, or insults often have shame at their roots. And because shame is linked to fear of disconnection, it's not easy to talk about those strong reactions, and keeping them a secret only gives shame more power over your life. Shame keeps you in a box because it keeps you believing that if people actually knew you or knew about your actions in the past, they wouldn't like you, and you'd be alone. I've been in that box plenty of times due to the fear of being judged unworthy. Hiding means survival, so we hide, we don't reveal anyth ɪg, and no one finds out about us. The problem with this, though, is that the n ɪre you hide your true self, the more suffering you'll experience, and the less ɔu'll feel joy, freedom, and peace in your life.

Reclaiming ur Power from Shame

To con licate life even more, shame is often a family dynamic we have learned to ı mic by watching parents or grandparents. But it's not a feeling you are stu with. Once you realize you are experiencing shame, you can change and ecome shame resilient by speaking about it out in the open, in a safe place, a meeting it with compassion and empathy rather than judgment.

I had tc arn this the hard way. I wasn't a huge fan of putting my real self out there. I fact, I spent decades trying to be what I thought other people wanted me ɔ be and concealing my real feelings and thoughts, which did nothing for ıy self-esteem or for getting what I really wanted in life. When you are not illed in this area, being vulnerable and authentic is terrifying and daunting at rst. When you finally decide to practice stepping into the light consistently evealing your unique gifts to this world, you will experience a huge weigh ifted off you and an energy that will fill you like no other.

So lear o express your true self and break through the illusion of fear that you're ı t good enough. Stop holding back, express your thoughts, ideas, opinions, a contributions, and share them with the world. It's healthy and powerful fc ɔur mental, emotional, and physical self.

CAUTION: If you trade in your authenticity for safety, you may experience the following: anxiety, depression, eating disorders, addiction, rage, blame, resentment, and inexplicable grief.
~Brené Brown, The Gifts of Imperfection

Sometimes I would share my feelings of shame with Brent, but his tendency was to go into fix-it mode and give me suggestions on how to get rid of it. When I finally came to the conclusion that his take wasn't right for me, I found empathy and shame resilience in my girlfriends Beth, Chris and Edna, who would listen to me cry and go on about what was happening. These great listeners met me with empathy, and my shame was defeated.

According to researcher Brené Brown, shame needs three things to thrive: secrecy, silence, and judgment (often self-imposed). In order to challenge shame and face it head on, only one of those three actions needs to be confronted to shift yourself from its grasp. Brown calls this shame resilience, and in order to achieve it, you need to have someone in your life willing to listen to your plight with empathy. It is this type of empathy that enables you to speak out your truth and reclaim your power from shame. This is why having a safe support community in your life is essential to making life changes. I've sought to create this type of community on Facebook so that anyone who joins can enjoy the benefits of having other women around who are willing to be real and provide the type of empathy needed to enable you to become shame resilient and unmessable. Please join our Facebook group called Be Unmessable! Community.

FOR YOUR JOURNAL

By understanding how your brain works, you have another key to being unmessable and handling what life throws at you. Take out your journal and find a comfortable place to sit. Take a few deep breaths, and spend some time reading through the following questions. Take your time to record your answers with as much detail as you need.

1. Think of something you are truly grateful for: an event, person, or thing. Really enjoy the gratitude you have for this and feel the goodness in your body from the gratitude. Why are you so grateful for this? How has this contributed to your life? Where in your body do you feel the gratitude?

2. Think about areas of your life where you recognize that you have been on autopilot. Describe two of your most common autopilot stories. Who are they about, or what are they about?

3. About what or whom in your life would you like to create a new story? About yourself? About an event? About a friend or relative?

4. What would this new story tell that would enable a new option to open in your life—that you didn't see before—and still be in alignment with your vision?

5. What story or stories do you need to let go of in order to experience something new?

6. Name the time or event that you now recognize as a point when your amygdala was hijacked.

7. When in life have you tried to hide something from others so that they didn't know the real you?

8. Who in your life could be a trusted confidant and be empathetic when talking about your shame? If you cannot think of anyone, please be sure to join our Be Unmessable! Community on Facebook so that you will have others who will show up for you with understanding.

9. What activities allow you to connect with yourself and be creative? How do you prefer to relax yourself?

CHAPTER TAKEAWAYS

1. Keeping your brain in a calm and peaceful state leads to being unmessable by opening the pathways to creativity and possibilities.

2. Check in with yourself when you are running on an autopilot story that isn't leading you where you need to go.

3. Check in with yourself to discover what needs you are attempting to fill with various behaviors. Intentionally change those behaviors that don't align with your vision and choose new behaviors that do align with your vision.

4. Find someone with whom you can be real and vulnerable, someone who will allow you to be shame resilient.

Chapter 8

ANOTHER WAY TO COMMUNICATE

THE WAY IN WHICH YOU COMMUNICATE is paramount to becoming unmessable. This is equally true for both internal and external communication. First, focus on shifting your internal conversations with yourself. Then external communication with others will become easier, and you will naturally radiate joy and love more abundantly in your relationships. Life is short, and your words need to be used wisely to get the most out of this one life you have been gifted.

INTERNAL COMMUNICATION

What you say and how you choose to communicate with yourself is extremely important and also has a direct impact on being unmessable. One thing is for certain: No matter what you say in life, people will challenge you; this you can count on. And although you need to challenge yourself when it comes to growing and changing, you always need to be your own biggest cheerleader.

Be Your Biggest Advocate

Notice what happens in your internal conversation when you make a mistake. Maybe you drop a favorite mug or are late to pick up one of your kids from school. Think of what you say under your breath that only you can hear. Are you self-critical and condemning with verbal attacks, or are you compassionate with patience and grace? Your internal conversation needs to be filled with understanding, grace, love, and forgiveness. Each of us has an inner child that we need to nurture and care for on a daily basis. You wouldn't call a four-year old "stupid." So you don't need to address your inner child, who hears everything you say as truth, that way either. Yes, you need to be mindful of how you speak to yourself and to that little child inside as a way to build yourself up, no matter the circumstance. This practice is essential.

Because your brain listens to all you say and develops your personal beliefs and patterns based on the information it takes in, you need to protect yourself from developing unsupportive, untrue, or harmful beliefs. Speak to yourself with kindness and compassion. If you don't forgive yourself, who will? Be your biggest advocate; you're counting on it.

More than anything you guard, protect your mind,
for life flows from it. ~Proverbs: 4:23

Choose Your Words Carefully

I'm sure you've heard the saying "If you don't have anything nice to say, then don't say anything at all." This also goes for when you talk to yourself. Just because someone acts in a thoughtless way doesn't mean that person is a thoughtless person. The same applies to doing something stupid; it doesn't mean that the person is stupid. This goes back to the subject of shame we talked about in chapter 7. We've all done things that we wish we could take back or aren't proud of, but these actions don't define who we are. They are only chapters in your book of life. So, be kind when speaking to yourself, including the manner in which you correct yourself.

People don't want to be judged or pigeonholed based on what they've done or said in the past. Things change, people change, and we grow and learn to see things differently as we mature. You've probably gone through tough times and learned tough lessons as you figured stuff out, but it's made you who you are today. Rehashing old stories, old mistakes, and old choices with judgment or condemnation based on one chapter of your life isn't helpful. Your worst chapter is not your whole book.

Don't call yourself names when speaking to yourself. There is only so much time in a day, and I guarantee name-calling is not in alignment with reaching any vision. According to *Webster's* Dictionary, name-calling is used to reject or condemn and there is no room for it on the path to becoming unmessable. Instead, for a life of joy, fun, abundance, and peace, call yourself names that are uplifting, and you may just get to your destination faster.

This point about being impeccable with your word is clearly illustrated in the book *The Four Agreements*. Author Ruiz talks about impeccable usage of the words you use with yourself. This means only using kind language so as not to prepare the fertile ground of your mind to accept name-calling from others. This practice of putting yourself down with names like "stupid," "idiot," and "poor" is nonnegotiable and the same is true for allowing anyone else to lord it over you with accusing power. If you replace the judgmental names with uplifting ones like "rock star," "genius," and "money magnet," imagine the difference it will make when you screw something up and blurt out, "Rock star! You forgot to pick up your kid!" This tactic interrupts the pattern and gives your brain a different path to take. At the very least, the interruptio will cause you to laugh or, at the most, to take a moment and learn from

What e ls up coming out of our mouths when we communicate to others begins inte ally, so it is essential to examine all you say to yourself and how you say it. (back and see how this relates to chapter 7, too, with respect to how the bra makes up stories about people and situations.

Abolish Ass ptions and Ask

Anothe old saying states, "Never 'assume'" because when you 'assume,' you make an 'as out of 'u' and 'me.'" Making assumptions is a practice you need to minimiz n order to be unmessable. As I explained previously, the brain makes assu ptions all the time about what people are doing and thinking, which can l d you to believe you know what is actually happening in other people's he s. Of course, sometimes this means that you will be correct, but sometimes u won't. Believing something is true doesn't make it so. The look on a person face may convey anger when actually that person could be deep in thought. r a person's sigh may signal irritation to you when it could be a release of nsion in a heart that's heavy. We humans make stuff up all the time; it's pa of being human, and it's how our brains fill in the gaps, just as they are des ned to do.

Assumi stuff about people and events also encourages miscommunication and ings on chaos. When you believe your assumption is the truth, chances are u will act out based on that perception. Remember, it's like looking through nses that are either clear or skewed. When you assume someone is angry an on't verify that assumption with the person, you never know if you are livi out a false narrative. Doing this regularly causes relationships to suffer unne ssarily. But if you take this a step forward and drop your assumption, you o n up a world of possibilities with amazing results.

In the f est, we did not have water hookups but instead used two blue, five-gallon ater jugs to dispense water through a small white spout. This amount of water was only enough for a day or two for a family of five. This meant going into town several times a week and finding water so we could fill the jugs. Paying for prefilled water jugs was not in our budget. We needed to find free water. Sometimes we could find a water spigot at a rest stop, trailhead, or park, and we usually had to drive a good distance to find that, which contradicted the concept of finding free water.

The gas station near our camping spot had a spigot on the outside of its building, and Brent suggested I ask the cashier if we could use it to fill up our jugs. Not only did I not want to ask, but I also was mortified to even go inside the store. My brain was dealing with the potential threat of the cashier saying no, calling me out for not having money, and rejecting me. In advance, I had harshly judged myself to deal with my shame. I concocted this story in my head and assumed the cashier knew we had no money and would judge us on that and throw us out. Brent went into the store himself, and the cashier happily agreed to let us fill up our jugs.

Your Thoughts Are Your Own

None of us can read minds, so why do we expect others to know what we are thinking? People sometimes hazard a lucky guess, but no one can read your mind, so don't assume anyone can. The danger here is that when you assume a person knows what you want or need, it causes hurt, abandoned, or sad feelings when that person doesn't deliver the way you expect. This is another way in which assuming creates unnecessary chaos and wasted energy and keeps you from becoming unmessable.

Your Internal Questions

The quality of your life is a direct reflection of the quality of the questions you are asking yourself. ~Anthony Robbins

---

As you become more mindful and notice what you say to yourself, you'll also notice what questions you ask yourself. You will be surprised as it becomes clear why people have trouble getting what they want in life; the questions they ask don't even get them on the same road, let alone the same lane, as their vision. If you say things like you want more joy and peace in your life but continue to ask yourself this—"What's wrong with you?"—you're making it impossible to get any traction on that road to your vision.

Becoming intentionally mindful of your internal talk and the questions you ask—and the questions you are afraid to ask yourself—is key to identifying what is keeping you stuck and not able to progress toward your vision. What are your fallback questions? Do they support you? If not, change them up!

Try this the next time you find yourself feeling stuck: Pause and take a moment and think about the questions you ask yourself that make you feel stuck. It's likely those questions are leading you directly to a stagnant place or a place of judgment, not to your vision. Questions like "Why does this always happen to me?" or "What's wrong with her?" only become self-fulfilling prophesies and a wedge in relationships—so stop asking them now!

Maximize the questions you ask yourself daily to direct yourself toward your vision and toward experiencing more positivity, gratitude, and joy. Questions such as "What am I most excited about?" "What do I most appreciate?" and "What can I do today to reach my vision sooner?" will employ your brain to direct you to your vision.

Once you become aware and skillful at this practice, you will be able to choose how you feel by changing the questions you ask yourself. Instead of experiencing anger when the car beside you cuts in front of you during your commute to work, you can choose to feel compassion by asking yourself, "I wonder what emergency this guy is trying to get to." It may seem crazy, but ultimately you have a choice. Questions like "What else could this mean?" and "How is this event working for my highest good?" will lead you back to your vision. Come up with several of these pocket questions so you are armed at all times with supportive ammo that directs you back on course. Your questions direct your focus, which needs to be on your vision, and they have a direct impact on how quickly you get to live the life you really want. It's up to you.

Keeping yourself focused takes practice, and when you get frustrated or off track, remember you're building your focus muscle, which takes some time and effort. Surround yourself with people who are practicing these same skills. It will prove you aren't the only one who needs practice. We all do. Join our Be Unmessable community and receive the support of other women who are becoming unmessable.

EXTERNAL COMMUNICATION

External conversations are often unconsciously arranged to set the participants up for a right-wrong debate. This is really only helpful if you enjoy debating and your conversation partner is willing to do it and is up for it. Ninety percent of the time these right-wrong conversations lead to arguments, division, and distance.

Reframing the Right-Wrong Conversation

When you allow others to express an opinion without argument, you open up an opportunity to lean in and get insight into the perspective of others. This is the opposite approach from being in a conversation with someone who gets defensive when you speak or tries to get you to think like he or she does.

This is not healthy communication. It's an attempt to prove the person right. Nothing about this interaction feels good, and it's another reason to ditch the right-wrong style of communicating.

This is the type of interaction that commonly happens online. So rather than getting into a right-wrong battle on social media when someone posts something you don't agree with, just lean into it and ask questions and get curious. It will disarm the person. You could ask people how they came to their opinions or why it is they feel so strongly about the subjects. Your curiosity and willingness to listen will bring people closer to you rather than separate you. These types of questions don't admit wrong; nor do they encourage agreement. The purpose of the questions is merely to open up an opportunity to learn more about people, exchange information, and connect, which is likely more in alignment with your vision.

Words That Don't Serve You

Small shifts in the words you choose to use will determine your perspective and cause large changes over time. The two words that change your perspective and attitude the quickest are the words *have to*. People use these words habitually, as in "I have to go to work," "I have to pick up the kids," or "I have to make dinner." A proper reframing of these phrases is "I get to go to work," or "I get to pick up my kids," or "I get to cook a meal." When I suggest these changes to my clients, some balk at first, feeling triggered at the idea that they *get to* do things they don't exactly enjoy. Remember, changing your words and perspective works for your benefit. These shifts in the way you talk to yourself are for you. Even though other people may benefit, this small shift in word selection greatly impacts how you experience life. Language is powerful, as it changes focus on an activity from a burden to a gift.

Look for areas in your life where you can change up your words and get closer to your vision. Considering household or work tasks as a gift enables you to see all the abundance you already have. Dirty dishes mean you have food on your table, work deadlines mean you have a job, and the pickup line at school means your children are being educated. Small shifts in your words make huge changes long-term.

Ask and you shall receive. ~ Matthew 7:7-8

Ask for What You Want

It's difficult to fairly judge any personal relationship if you haven't given the other person a chance to know what you want. This also creates unnecessary suffering in your own life—when you assume that people know what you want but aren't giving it to you. Instead, ask specifically for what you want.

Asking for what you want was a big lesson for me to learn. I used to assume people knew what I needed or wanted. My parents and sisters provided most of my wants and needs as a child without me having to ask. When I became an adult, I just assumed my boyfriend and eventually my husband knew too, but he didn't. As Brent always told me, he didn't have a crystal ball, and I needed to ask for what I wanted, as you do. But asking makes many of us feel vulnerable and scared. We fear the unknown answer or the ridicule for simply asking the question, so we build a case that if they loved us, they should already know. This typical autopilot brain response can be changed, so keep reading and you'll see how.

I need some help, could you . . . ?

Would you help me, please?

Could I get some of your help?

It's the Brain's Fault!

The stories and beliefs we develop about the world often inhibit us from being able to ask for what we want or need. Remember, it's how the brain physically operates. Part of becoming unmessable is about not only exploring the physical reasons but also the beliefs that hold us back.

One of my clients, Barb, was scared to ask her partner for relief when it came to getting help running errands. She was feeling taken advantage of, as she needed time to look for full-time work. We explored her beliefs, and that helped her realize she believed she wasn't allowed to question or decline her partner's requests to run all the errands because she wasn't the breadwinner. She identified this belief in a way that made her decide it no longer served her, and that identification gave her the courage to simply ask for what she needed. She is unmessable.

Clarification

Minimizing assumptions requires asking for more clarification. In any relationship, personal or business, when someone says something that makes you go, "Huh?"—ask a quick question like, "Oh, how so?" Try this. Voice a polite, quick ask for a little more clarification. This allows you to dispel your assumptions and get to the real heart of what is being said, saving time and energy and saving you from the suffering of the unknown. By not attempting to fill in those blanks yourself, you may be pleased by the answer.

When your partner behaves in a way that makes you think he or she is angry or frustrated or irritated, ask about it. Keep it simple, clarify what you are feeling, and see if you are correct. Make it clear that you don't want to assume anything and are inquiring to help deepen your understanding and mutual connection. Asking for clarification enables you to get what you need to form a better understanding of what is really taking place in your conversations, and it gets you closer to your vision.

INSTEAD OF ASSUMING,

CLARIFY WITH
A QUESTION

ARE YOU ANGRY WITH ME?
I DON'T WANT TO ASSUME. DO YOU MEAN...?
OH, HOW SO?

BUILD ONE ANOTHER UP

In order to create opportunities in all types of circumstances and be unmessable, start with learning to build people up. It may seem irrelevant to creating opportunities, but focusing understanding, compassion, and grace on others will undoubtedly draw others toward connection with you and teach you also to be more compassionate with yourself.

This is the same process as gossiping, only positive. Yes, the habit of gossiping and talking about other people is also a source of connection, but it usually involves complaining. I used to complain about my marriage as a way of connecting with my girlfriends, but building someone up is a more powerful way to connect with friends and family while living within your vision.

If you remember in chapter 7, we learned about the six human needs and how contribution was one of the two essentials for a life of fulfillment. Contribution fulfills an amazing part of our human needs in that we don't have to contribute, but when we do, it feels amazing not only to the person receiving the contribution but also to the one contributing. It's a total win-win!

Building others up is a type of contribution. So use a portion of the 16,000 average words we speak each day to build others up and feel incredible! Imagine the difference you can make in one person's day just by smiling and saying something uplifting. I'm not talking about schmoozing or giving fake compliments; I'm talking about recognizing the good in others and pointing it out. This type of communication will change your life forever.

I've learned that people will forget what you said, people will forget what you did, but people will never forget how you made them feel. ~ Maya Angelou

---

One part of my vision for life is to love people unconditionally, though I must admit that some days I'm better at it than others. I do consciously think about how I can love others. This goes for both my friends and family as well as the people I encounter during the normal course of my day in both my business and personal life.

Try it! The next time you go to the store, think consciously about projecting love to every person you come in contact with. Maybe it will take the form of a smile or asking people how their day is going or projecting toward them an open, loving energy about you. Any way to choose to do it, you'll be adding value and joy to someone else's life, and it just plain feels good to do it. Plus, it keeps you and your brain in a positive place, working toward having a more spectacular life. Be sure to also include some self-love and appreciation in this building up!

Nonverbal communication

Nonverbal communication is accomplished without ever saying a word, is very effective, and can either be positive or negative. I'm sure you've experienced it yourself. This is the energy you pick up from others when you walk into a room. What you feel might be the residual energy of an argument with a coworker or perhaps a couple who finished up a loving phone interaction, and you might feel the sparks flying.

The bottom line is that we communicate in many ways, and many do not involve speaking. Our facial expression, body movement, posture, touch, and eye contact can also say so much to the world. This is an essential part of communication that you must be aware of. It's important because even when you are saying yes to a request, your whole body language and energy may be saying no. Making sure your body, mind, and mouth are in alignment is crucial to great relationships.

In the past, I would sometimes, though reluctantly, say yes to my husband's requests for help in the garage, and he would end up saying to me that my words were saying one thing but everything else on my body was saying the opposite. My eye contact was dismissive, my body language was stiff, and I wasn't bringing good energy to the task. I didn't want to be there, and he knew it.

Your senses have to be in alignment to communicate effectively and truthfully! Let your yes be yes and your no be no. If you don't want to help someone out or cannot make the time because you have something else planned, then say no. It's OK to say no. After all, you aren't rejecting the requester as a person; you are only declining to share a task. Saying no does not mean you do not love the person. It just means you are a priority in your own life. It's up to you to take care of you.

Say Yes to Saying No!

Many of my clients and women I've mentored have told me that they have felt uncomfortable saying no to loved ones, and they've always felt compelled to help out when asked. If your sister requests help moving on a day you planned to get some much-needed rest, or a friend asks you to lie on the friend's behalf and it's not in alignment with your beliefs, say no. You can always say no without guilt and with no need to apologize. Learning to say no is also a way of taking care of yourself. It is as important as any other appointment or meeting. Think of it as a meeting with yourself to keep yourself in alignment with your vision for your life, which is why there is nothing to apologize for.

The outcome, though, can cause disagreement, anger, or disappointment. Hear out the other person's feelings, which you cannot control and aren't responsible for. That allows the person to feel those feelings. Their feelings belong to them and yours to you. No one is required to feel happy about your no, but the requester does need to respect your answer.

Saying No Is Easier When You're Honest

You need to be honest about your feelings, and you need to be in line with your agreements. Otherwise, your answer comes out sideways and doesn't ring true. That's when you find yourself slipping into an argument or answering in a snappy voice. For instance, you might feel cornered and don't really want to do the thing requested, but you don't know how to say no without feeling awful. To avoid this type of situation, start by understanding that you are not responsible for being at another person's beck and call. You have your own life.

Here are some loving ways to decline requests:

1. I love you, and I can't show up for that this weekend.

2. I want you to feel supported because I love you and I don't feel comfortable doing that. Is there something different I can do to support you?

3. I already have plans on Thursday; can we make it a different day?

4. I have to say no to that.

5. That is not going to happen.

6. No.

IMPORTANT CONVERSATIONS

What follows are discussions about two conversations that we've all had. You might not have even been aware that these conversations have held you back in life, but they have, so read on. Knowing how they impact your life and how to change them will enable you to become unmessable.

The Scarcity Conversation

This type of conversation is engaged in daily, and it promotes dialogues that keep the participants small, the opposite of being unmessable. Don't let this be you! Your conversations need to match your vision. Speaking words like "I can't afford it," "I don't make enough," or "I never get what I want" are small and keep you in a place of scarcity when, in actuality, you have quite a bit of abundance.

I recall being reminded of a passage by an unknown author, while we were struggling and homeless. It stated that if you have food in the refrigerator, clothes on your back, a roof over your head, and a place to sleep, then you are richer than 75 percent of the people in this world. If you have money in the bank, or in your wallet, or spare change in a dish someplace, then you are among the top eight percent of the world's wealthy. If you can read a list like this, then you don't belong to the one billion people who cannot read. This reminder was a godsend, because even though we were homeless, we had food, clothes, spare change, opportunities, healthy brains, bodies and love of one another.

It is highly important to have impeccable word choice. When you say that you can't afford something, you also plant that same thought in your brain and strengthen that negative pathway. Negative pathways become ruts, and like a muddy country road, they are difficult to travel. Instead, train yourself to be specific and accurate when choosing words. Of course you can afford to buy some of what you want, but perhaps you haven't made some purchases a priority or haven't learned to ask the most productive questions, such as, How can I afford to buy that? or Where can I find the means to acquire that? If you make enough for a certain lifestyle but are looking to upgrade, say so. And, yes, you do get what you want, but now you are committed to a new vision and want something else. Likewise, choose words that propel you forward toward your vision, empower you, and positively impact your perspective about what you currently have.

Value Conversation

The value conversation is an internal dialogue that raises the question, When will I be enough? It usually comes up when a person feels rejected, abandoned, or lonely. Maybe it's after a breakup, job loss, or long period of being alone. I once heard at a training seminar that it's a conversation that occurs in the heads of 80 percent of all women. You ask these questions: Am I valuable? Do I matter? Am I enough? Yes, yes, and yes you are!

There's nothing wrong with being humble, but if you want to be unmessable, you need to stop devaluing yourself. You know you are meant for more! When you devalue yourself, your opinion doesn't feel like it is worth much, so perhaps you fail to give your opinion at a work meeting, are reluctant to tell your partner how you really feel unless the partner brings up an issue first, allow others to control your decisions, and are hesitant to proclaim your accomplishments. This diminishing behavior can be tough to change because you and the people you surround yourself with are so accustomed to your hiding your true value.

When you do shift to start showing the world who you really are, there are those who may try to minimize, criticize, or judge you. They haven't walked in your shoes; nor have they lived your exact life. So, they do not have the exact context in which to accurately judge you. Any judgement or criticism they dish out should be automatically negated in your head. It's completely their opinion, subjective, and should be treated as neutral information.

Knowing you have true value, just as you are, translates to self-worth. The debate that goes on inside your head, skeptical of your value, is not a conversation that is up for discussion. You are worthy. But first, you need to believe it about yourself. Although we attempt to get others to fill that void of belief in us, it's not up to them or what they say. It's up to us to believe we are worth it. Trying to do everything perfectly will not prove to you that you are worthy. You need to believe me here. You must choose to believe that no matter what anyone has ever said to you, you are valuable. According to Dr. Ali Binazir, when you consider the probabilities of your parents meeting, staying together long enough to have children, and so on, the odds of you being born into this world as *you* are about zero. You are an incredible phenomenon!

There are over 7.5 billion people in the world, and no two of us are totally identical, not even twins. We have our own unique spin on things, perspectives, experiences, interactions, and beliefs. We are all unique, with our own unique story. This also makes us rare, and when something is rare, it is valuable—instantly! An original is what you are!

You are like a one-of-a-kind priceless piece of art, so treat yourself the same way. If someone came along and tried to convince you that priceless artwork was worthless or less than priceless, you would laugh and not believe it. So why would you undervalue yourself when you know that you are also rare and priceless? You are a true gem with unlimited value!

As you begin to blossom into all of who you are, of course some people will feel discomfort. It's normal. Humans tend to like their comfort zones since they keep the brain feeling safe. When you change and shift, others will feel it and may want you to shrink back so they don't feel uncomfortable and feel the need to change. As American author Marianne Williamson says, "There is nothing enlightened about shrinking so that other people won't feel insecure around you."

When you embrace that you are valuable, your life will transform before your eyes! That's why you need to use words that align with your tremendous, unique value. You will be amazed to see how this small shift has a huge impact! Words are powerful!

FOR YOUR JOURNAL

Now that you understand how important internal and external communication are to being unmessable, take out your journal and find a comfortable place to sit. Take a few deep breaths, spend some time reading through the following questions, and take time to write down your answers to the questions in as much detail as you need.

1. Think of a conversation you've had recently in which you were triggered by what the other person said. Detail that conversation in your journal. Next, ask yourself what assumptions you made during the conversation and write them down, including how you could have better clarified any points or what questions you could have asked to better understand what was being discussed.

2. For one week, take notice of the questions you are asking yourself when feeling low. Log them in your journal. I started you on the low questions, because as humans, it is easier for us to notice when we feel low. It's a brain thing. Then the following week take notice and log the questions you ask yourself when you are feeling awesome!

3. Write down three intentional questions to ask yourself each morning and three each evening that will bring you closer to your vision. The questions may be the same or different for morning and evening. It's up to you to decide what will lead you best to your vision.

4. Contemplate the following questions, remembering that asking powerful questions causes physical changes in your brain, and reflect how the recalled situations influenced your life. Record your answers.

    - What are some of the most fun times I've had in life?

- When have I felt extremely loved?
- What is one of my most proud memories?
- What am I grateful for?
- What are my highest blessings in life?
- What do I appreciate most in life right now?

5. What words do you usually use when you put yourself down? Write them in your journal. Now come up with uplifting words you will use from now on. Write them down and practice them daily.

6. Then think of ten things that are great about you and ten things you love and value about yourself and write them in your journal.

7. Pretend you are up for auction at a charity event and you have to describe to the audience why its members should be the highest bidder for priceless, unique you! Write a short description of why you are so amazing.

8. Think about a scarcity conversation or phrase you recognize you've had with yourself in the past. Write it in your journal. Where did you get this conversation or phrase? Write it down. Now flip it and write a new conversation. Example of a scarcity phrase: "We can't afford it." I heard my mom say this phrase a bunch when I was a child. Example of a new approach: "How can I afford this thing I want?"

CHAPTER TAKEAWAYS

1. Instead of assuming you know what someone means, ask the person to clarify by asking questions.

2. Becoming aware of self-talk and what you regularly ask yourself is a huge key to being unmessable.

3. Ask yourself the questions that can best get you closer to what you actually want in life, questions that are in alignment with your vision.

4. Always guard your heart and speak to yourself kindly. It's nonnegotiable!

5. Choose your words carefully.

6. You are a rare gem and priceless!

Chapter 9

ANOTHER WAY TO LISTEN

THINK OF WHAT IT WOULD BE LIKE to hear anything being said without it throwing you off course. Not only is this possible, but I will also show you how to fine-tune your listening in such a way as to become unmessable. You learned how your brain thinks in chapter 7, and in this chapter you will learn how the brain is greatly influenced by what you hear. What you hear is what the brain processes to create the beliefs and autopilot programs needed to protect you. This means it's important to be conscious and intentional about the following: what you allow yourself to listen to, how you assign meanings to what you hear, and ways to strengthen and hone the listening ability of your built-in guidance system.

LISTEN UP!

Your brain and mind are fertile ground that need to be nourished with the information to make decisions, choices, and beliefs that align with your vision for life. Becoming unmessable requires you to intentionally align your listening environment with your vision.

My kids think I am being ridiculous when I don't want to listen to their music choices. Like many of you, I hate it when a song melody or lyric gets stuck in my head, especially if it's one like "you a stupid hoe" or "b**ch" or "gold digger." That's not to imply I never listen to songs that have interesting lyrics, because I often do, especially when I can dance to them, but what I am saying is that making a conscious choice about what is allowed into your brain on a regular basis is very important.

To be the gatekeeper of what you allow your brain to process, you must first become acutely aware of what you now allow your brain to hear. There is so much noise around, and we are assaulted by so much in the way of music (ours and other people's), as well as the words we hear from television show hosts, actors, newscasters, politicians, podcasters, religious leaders, and other people. Every choice we make has an impact on the brain. The brain absorbs it all, sometimes with a negative impact that you don't even notice until you become anxious or change how you view yourself, others, or the world. The brain is a sponge. Just marvel at how you can repeat lines from movies and lyrics from songs without ever consciously memorizing them.

Take Inventory

To be unmessable, you need to first take inventory of what you listen to and take notice of how many of those external sources of sound are actually aligned with your life vision. If your vision is all about joy, then listening to newscasters spewing fear and division won't allow you to fully express or experience the joy of living. You also need to take notice of all the people you listen to (in media and in your personal life) and notice how many are aligned with the same things you want for your life, your vision. This ability to assess what you allow your brain to hear, along with the ability to utilize it to make conscious decisions as to what you actually retain, follow, or change is how you gain new experiences to attain your vision. Quite simply, this means listening more to the people, media, and music that align with your vision and avoiding those sources, either for long periods or altogether, that don't. Because life is short, it is important to remember to act accordingly and shorten the time to reach your life vision.

AM I HEARING WHAT I THINK I'M HEARING?

The brain assigns meaning to what it hears with the information stored in its memory bank. This memory bank is the repository of all your past experiences. This means that if you want to be unmessable, you must challenge the status quo by becoming aware of the meanings you might be unconsciously assigning to your conversations. The advantage to being able to do this is to allow you to distinguish between the language you use that aligns with and gets you closer to your vision and the language that doesn't—along with the ability to choose differently.

Triggers (Also Known As External Factors That Press Your Buttons)

You've probably experienced an instant emotional or physical reaction resulting from something said to you either directly or indirectly. This is a trigger. Maybe you've experienced a trigger after hearing a politician making another false claim on a breaking news story, when a drunk family member says you don't know what you're talking about at Thanksgiving, or when someone posts a mean tweet about one of your kids. (This is one trigger that hijacks the amygdala with great efficiency and that sends mama bear directly into fighting mode.)

Stop People from Pressing Your Buttons

To become unmessable, you need to acquire the ability to short-circuit triggers by not allowing people or circumstances to mess you up in the first place. The following three-step process is to be learned and implemented whenever you feel triggered. The secret is to recognize the feeling that signals you're being triggered. With practice, you will be able to reroute your triggered state by taking a couple of seconds to pause and then choose the path that aligns with your vision. Here's how:

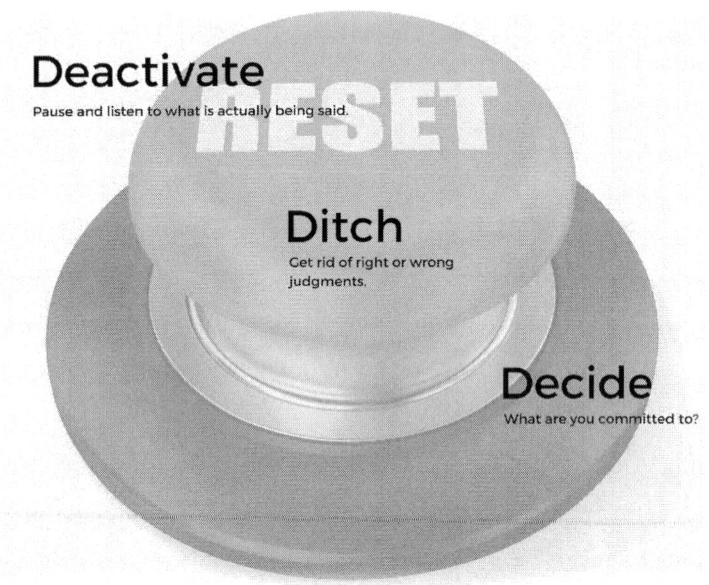

Step 1. Deactivate the button

When you get that first inkling of being in a triggered state, register that feeling and immediately pause all action. Exhale the air from your lungs and stop there—do not breathe for four seconds. Then inhale slowly for four seconds and stop there—do not breathe for four seconds. Next, breathe out slowly for four seconds. What this does is focus your attention on your breathing, which helps you to connect with yourself and that, in turn, relaxes both body and mind, freeing your brain to function at its best rather than while its reacting automatically. Do not practice this while you are driving.

It is at this stage that you must listen for only what is actually being said to you by the other person. Take the emotion out of what you heard. Repeat that other person's statement to yourself and listen to it as if its neutral information being spoken by a reporter, not the person who actually spoke those words to you. Hearing these words spoken by a reporter as if reporting on an event essentially neutralizes the information and lets you objectively decide what you want to do with it. This practice is incredibly powerful and essential for making better connections with people and improving relationships. It may take a little while to get good at it, but when you master it, it's priceless since you save yourself from the tailspin of emotion. Deactivating the button shortens the length of time you spend in a triggered state, thereby lessening the intensity of the trigger. This practice gets the brain back to a relaxed and creative state fast, allowing you to think of other possibilities to connect in your conversation or relationship.

Step 2. Ditch the Right-Wrong

When people voice their perspectives and their opinions, always try to remember that they are based on their experience on this planet and that those perspectives and opinions are not necessarily also true for you. Bottom line: You don't have to agree with someone to get along with that person. Feedback, perspective, and opinion are neither right nor wrong; they are neutral. It is information based on someone else's experience, so do not get defensive. When your disagreement puts the other person on the defensive, a discussion becomes a competition, as you've prejudged the other person wrong so you can feel right or justified, as if you've won. This always results in a hollow win, as the winning feeling is not real and does not last or bring people together. Instead of a win, it is really a type of resistance, and it only creates more tension, problems, and triggers. Taking the "I'm right and you're wrong" stance is not the foundation on which relationships are built. But when you take out the right-wrong, win-lose paradigm, the discussion becomes neutral, allowing you both to make choices and voice opinions, thereby deepening your relationship.

The paradox here is that the people who trigger us most often are those with whom we are closest and care about the most deeply. This simple rule of ditching the right-wrong is a great way to keep the lines of communication open and remain on the same side in union with those you love.

Opinion and Perspective Are Neutral Unless You Take Them Personally

We are all allowed to have our own personal opinion and perspective. But when you ask another person for feedback, and that person gives you an honest answer that might be not what you expected, what is neutral to the provider of the feedback may come across as either a positive or negative to you (depending on how you interpret it). But that doesn't make it so. When it's an opinion or perspective you are asking for, consider the feedback neutral. As it says in *Webster's Dictionary*, an opinion is a view or judgment formed about something and it is not necessarily based on fact or knowledge.

Consider online posts where the comments are piled on, with some people really liking the post and others definitely hating it, and don't forget about those who are undecided. Each person's opinion is of equal value. It's not personal; it's not about you. And, most importantly, it's not something you can control (so don't try to and make yourself crazy). However, if what is posted is a fact, then you have two choices: either accept it and own up by making a change for a more positive outcome or leave it alone.

In his 1997 book, *The Four Agreements*, author Don Miguel Ruiz states that one agreement is to not take anything personal, as to do so is a very selfish act in that you are making the assumption that everything is about you. No one but you knows what it's like to have lived your life or had your experiences, so others won't have your same perspective. Even people you love, who know your story, your triggers, your hurts and pains, still don't fully know what it is like in your world. Everyone has his or her own point of view, perspective, and opinions based totally on evidence gleaned from personal experience, childhood, past environment, and personal history. When you don't take the opinions of others personally, you will always be immune from any garbage comments they spew.

Then, of course, there are times when the opinions and perspectives of others are actually helpful (if you don't take them personally). When it's information someone is sharing that permits or opens a path, so that you get a different perspective of the subject, then I urge you not to give up this opportunity to learn. You'll recognize when an opportunity like this presents itself if you can just pause, breathe, and listen to what is actually being said as a neutral statement.

In the Bible, the four books of the New Testament are referred to as the Gospels, and in them four different individuals describe the same events from four different perspectives. Many of us have grown up reading and studying these Gospels, and I'm sure that, like me, you've never heard anyone say, "Oh no, Mark was wrong. Matthew's version was accurate," or "John was right, but Luke must have been on meds or something." Instead, we allow for and respect that each has his own unique take on how things played out and why. In fact, having these four accounts allows all readers of the Bible to gain the broadest sense of actual events from that time. The differences actually allow us to see and hear the situation from various angles and viewpoints. As multiple eyewitness accounts to the same event vary, sometimes greatly, interviewing everyone who saw or heard something serves to give the most complete picture of what actually happened and better decisions based on that more complete picture. I believe that when people verbalize their opinions, it's great for me because I often learn something new about them, about myself, and possibly about gaining a new perspective on a subject I hadn't yet considered.

Now all that's left to do is to get rid of the residual tension left from the fall-out of the trigger being activated and take your listening skills to the next level.

Step 3. Decide to Refocus

The years have given me plenty of practice getting triggered by the things my husband has said to me. He gives me that gift of practice. Most recently he came to me declaring that I was being unsupportive—something I hated to hear. This time, this comment particularly triggered lots of emotion and tension. Once I became aware of my triggered state, I paused to breathe, listened in a neutral way for what was actually being said, and ditched the right-wrong and personal assumptions I was muttering to myself. But somehow I still felt stressed.

I was momentarily freaking out, so to help me pop out of that state, I asked myself questions so that I could refocus and get back on a positive track. The type of question you need to ask in this situation can be something as simple as "What can I learn from this?" Asking yourself this type of question gives your brain a directive, an objective—a target for refocus. You need to be taken out of that bubble of tension, and refocusing pops a hole in it so all of that pressure can escape and blow out. Then your energy goes into answering that question: "What can I learn from this?" If that particular question doesn't fit your situation, substitute another one that works for you, such as "What is great about this?" or "How can I help somebody else with this?" By giving your brain a place to go, a place where it can function as it makes use of the energy generated from your pent-up frustration, your focus will shift, your body will relax, and you will feel better. Those feelings of resentment or tension will dissipate.

Always think about your life vision when you are in a situation like this. Recalling your vision makes it is easier to hear what is actually being said, and then you can interpret the meaning that best supports the attainment of your vision. When Brent said I was being unsupportive, instead of getting defensive or fighting back, I remembered my vision for my marriage was one of joy and union, so I refocused and heard his comment as neutral information. This choice helped me understand what he was experiencing and helped me realize that within that comment was some truth and some things I could do to help him feel more supported. Being open to accepting healthy feedback gives you an opportunity to make positive changes and an opportunity to assess and maybe decide that even if we don't agree with the feedback we're getting, we can still listen to another's opinion without needing to control it.

To be unmessable, choose to listen to feedback through a neutral prism and with understanding and curiosity.

INTUITIVE LISTENING

Humans possess a powerful inner guidance system—intuition. This remarkable ability, also called the sixth sense, is an awesome power as it is, but it can also be strengthened as you increase your ability to tap into it by learning to listen to what it is telling you. Learn to do this, and you expand your repertoire of skills that lead to being unmessable.

Intuition comes from a spiritual source that is alive within you and at the ready to assist you in reaching your vision. This inner guidance system has been referred to through the ages as the universe, the Holy Spirit, the sixth sense, a gut feeling, intuition, and a multitude of other names. Any way you choose to refer to it needs to account for its power to give meaning to uncertainty with an all-knowing ability to believe in yourself with the faith that you have exactly what you need within you, for any purpose, at any moment. Choose the one that feels right for you. My personal belief is that we are all created by a power greater than ourselves and that we are connected to one another by and through the love of our divine creator, who is always available for love and guidance. But you don't have to believe what I believe to experience this innate feeling of knowing you have the ability to intuit what you need to get you through anything life throws at you.

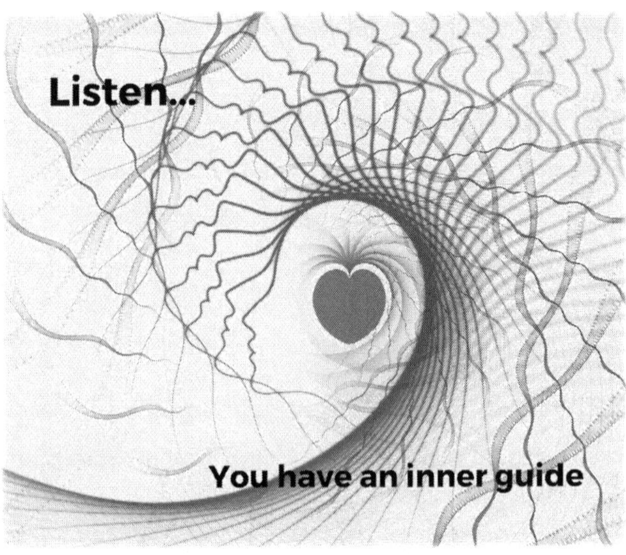

Years ago, I came upon the realization there was a very real guiding force in my life, and I hadn't been paying enough attention to what I was hearing. My guide would show up in the form of a nudge or a tap on the shoulder, with a quiet whisper. When we were camping, I still remember those nudges and the whispers in my ear: "Write the book." That's also when I really became more mindful of the lessons we were learning from the experiences we were having and their effect on our family. It was when I started viewing this experience through the lens of writing a book and when I started to see how our coping in this situation would help others that living became more bearable and, in fact, more fun. Because I chose to listen to the nudges and whispers of my guiding force, I was able to glean lessons from my experience to help other women who were going through the trials and tribulations of their own challenges. It gave a purpose to my struggle, knowing that by being resilient I was also teaching my children to be the same and, by extension, could also empower other women. The more I paid attention to what I heard, the easier it was to tap into my intuition and reap the benefits of what it was communicating to me.

I urge you to develop a strong relationship with your inner guidance system in the same way. It can only guide you if you are able to feel the nudges and hear the whispers. Learn to notice the nudges and whispers and then test them in ways to help you understand what they mean and how your inner guidance communicates with you. Our creator built us with an inherent ability to form relationships, including the one we have with the creator—the one who guides us. If you are wondering how to develop a relationship with an entity you cannot see, simply begin as you would in any relationship. Think of how a relationship develops. Spend time and effort getting to know likes and dislikes, make an effort to integrate this new being into your life, and listen for the inner voice that tells you how your union is now intertwined in some way. You just make a space in your life to listen to that still, small voice inside yourself and get used to knowing what to listen for and develop an ability to trust in it. Learn to do this, and you will benefit in ways you never thought possible from this immense inner resource. Those without an interest in tapping into this resource are saying no to receiving a gift from a source with a much broader perspective of the world who truly knows you and how much you need this gift.

To begin your relationship with your inner guide, imagine your guide is sitting in the passenger seat as you drive to work or perhaps is sitting with you while you drink your morning tea. Spend time with your guide, get to know her or him, ask questions, and then listen for the answers. Remember, there are no dumb questions. Your guide can accept your craziest venting sessions, pent-up anger, and sobs. Jot down in your journal what you hear your guide saying and make a special note of any prompts or suggestions. Also, write down what happens in your daily life after your guide makes certain suggestions. Do any themes emerge? Tracking what you learn about your intuition and the guidance you now have will help you to trust what you are being told and to trust the guidance coming your way so you can reap its benefits.

After you put out a request for guidance, you must be willing to listen for it. Otherwise you're only venting. Developing your intuition means that you must give yourself time and space and the faith to sit for an undesignated amount of time in uncertainty as you give yourself permission to explore your options. Instead of rushing into a decision, quiet your brain, open the bandwidth, listen for guidance, and feel the nudges and taps on the shoulder and any other signs that are sent to you. It may be tough at first to quiet your brain and hear the guidance, but it will get easier. If it's not happening fast enough for you, don't rush it. After you feel you've spent enough time, don't give up. Just do it again tomorrow. This is a form of meditation. It takes practice, and you must hone your senses as well as the ability to get quiet enough to hear what your guide is saying to you. The first sign you've succeeded will be when your fears seem to slip away. This will free you to connect to something bigger than yourself that will become your endless resource of strength and abundance. You will also realize that you were never alone; you just didn't know it.

We were never abandoned during our crisis even though I felt like we were. Once I took notice, I saw and felt evidence of God's guidance, humor, and gifts all around us.

Once you learn to tap into your intuitive powers, you will see that you have everything you need within you already. You only need to learn how to pull it out to become unmessable.

Ways to Improve Your Intuition

- Be *you*! Surround yourself with people who inspire you to be *all* you were created to be! When you constantly work to get the approval of those who prefer you to be someone you aren't, you won't have enough energy left to connect to that small voice of intuition.
- Choose *gratitude*! Keep yourself in a joyful and grateful state. If you spend a bunch of time and energy on difficult emotions, you won't be in a mode to get in touch with your intuition easily. Let go of the negative emotions that cloud your vision and cause you to make choices that keep you stuck.
- Be *present* and *notice*! Listen not only to what people are saying out loud but also to how they are saying it. Tone is important. Pay careful

attention also to body language and what a person projects through eye contact (or the lack thereof). Understanding that communication is done not only with words enables you to strengthen intuition skills.

- Be silent and *still.* Every day allow yourself to take a break from the demands of your day and tune into your intuition. If you are always in go, go, go mode and don't take a break to listen, you will miss out on the cautions and reassurance that your intuition often gifts to you.
- Ask and *surrender*! Whether it's prayer or meditation. Take the time to ask the Divine for help, for the answers you desire, and for the ability to hear the guidance. Then pause and listen to what comes up for you: feelings, thoughts, guidance.

FOR YOUR JOURNAL

Now that you understand how to expand your listening skills, take out your journal and find a comfortable place to sit. Take a few deep breaths, spend some time reading through the following questions, and then write down your answers with as much detail as you need.

1. How do you feel when someone says something untrue about you?

    a. What is a common response you have?

    b. Do you get defensive and try to control that person's opinion?

    c. How could you hear that person's perspective differently and respond differently?

    d. Write a few sentences about any defensiveness you've recently experienced and where you think it came from.

    e. How might you have responded if you had heard that person's perspective in a different voice, like one from a cartoon character or a little child?

    f. Why or what do you think prompted that person to say these things about you? Set aside your initial thoughts.

2. Journal about a time when you have been highly triggered or a future time when you suspect you are likely to experience a trigger. Record every detail of the experience, including what the person usually says, what it means to you, how you feel inside, and how you tend to react. Now rewrite that story through this three-step process.

- Deactivate—pause and listen as a neutral reporter to what the person actually said. Write down any realizations.
- Ditch any right or wrong judgments. Decide what vision you are committed to in life.
- Given your vision, is there an alternative way you could have viewed this situation. How else could you have responded? Listen for any understanding as to what that person was trying to get you to hear. How might that other person be feeling?

3. Take several deep breaths and relax. Picture yourself in a beautiful, peaceful, safe place. Think of three things you are grateful for in your life. Thank the Divine for all that you have been given and all that is to come. Say these words quietly to yourself: "Show me the love in my life. I surrender my ways. Please guide me." Ask your inner guide where your focus needs to be today and then spend a few minutes quietly listening to thoughts, feelings, and knowledge that arises. Jot down any notes about what comes up for you during your reflection time, and notice any themes or guidance that you may be receiving. Keep detailed notes about this experience. Practice this exercise daily, and keep notes about what you notice or any themes that come up.

CHAPTER TAKEAWAYS

1. Align your listening environment with your vision for your life.

2. Take inventory of what you listen to and notice how many of your sources are aligned with what you want for your life, your vision

3. Stop people from pressing your buttons using the three-step approach—deactivate, ditch, decide.

4. Practice to improve your intuition skills to better hear your divine inner guidance.

Chapter 10

ANOTHER WAY TO EMPOWER

SOMETIMES THE ENTIRE TRAJECTORY of your life can hinge on how you make a single decision. This chapter will show you how to tap into the power of your commitments, your personal responsibility, and your mindset, which is the real power behind controlling circumstances life throws at you and where you become unmessable.

When external influences took over my life, I felt hopeless. I wasn't aware I had a choice in the matter, and it seemed like I was a helpless ball in life's pinball machine, getting knocked around with no control. It was awful. When someone said something annoying to me, I felt annoyed for days, and when life threw stuff at me, I was knocked down for weeks. Then I discovered that I had way more power and control over what was happening to my life, and it all started with my commitment.

COMMITMENT

Until one is committed, there is hesitancy, the chance to draw back, always ineffectiveness. Concerning all acts of initiative (and creation), there is one elementary truth, the ignorance of which kills countless ideas and splendid plans: that the moment one definitely commits oneself, then providence moves too. All sorts of things occur to help one that would never otherwise have occurred. A whole stream of events issues from the decision, raising in one's favor all manner of unforeseen incidents and meetings and material assistance, which no man could have dreamt would have come his way. I have learned a deep respect for one of Goethe's couplets: whatever you can do, or dream you can, begin it. Boldness has genius, power, and magic in it. ~W.H. Murray

---

Think back to a time you wanted to try something new or make a change in your life, but then life started messing with you and nothing changed. Chances are you weren't committed to fully making a change, and in hindsight it may have been a good thing or maybe not. Recall the journal entry for chapter 6, where you came up with a vision of what you wanted for your life in specific areas at this particular time in our world. I'm here to tell you that if you really want this vision to come to fruition, you can do it if you are committed.

When I talk about commitment to a vision, I'm talking about dedicating yourself to that vision, declaring, promising, and obligating yourself to stand for, believe in, and reach for it and not let anyone or anything get in your way. It is this high level of commitment that you need to empower you to be unmessable, nothing less.

Your Current Commitment

It's easy to recognize your commitments when you take a personal inventory of your life.

- Where do you spend the most time, effort, and money?
- What always gets your attention?

Perhaps you are committed to your spouse, your children, your business, your TV shows, your addiction, your health, Facebook, or Instagram. When you notice where you spend the most time, effort, and money and see what gets addressed or attended to no matter what, the commitments that are already in place show themselves. After a simple inventory and comparison to what is currently being focused on, you'll know if your desires are only wishes and hopes or if they are, in fact, commitments.

Commitment to a Vision Can Change History

There are countless examples of this level of commitment in history. Harriet Tubman was committed to freeing enslaved people through the underground railroad after she escaped to freedom herself. Many told her it was too dangerous because of external influences, like armed slave owners, but she was committed, and nothing was going to get in her way.

Oskar Schindler was committed to protecting the lives of as many Jewish people as he could during World War II. External influences, Nazis, pressured him to be hateful and to exclude the Jewish people, but he was committed to saving them from impending doom.

John Hancock and Samuel Adams spoke up courageously and declared that all British soldiers should be ejected from Boston in 1774. That commitment resulted in the Declaration of Independence in 1776, and the two were charged with treason by the British monarchy. That powerful opposition could have stopped them, but they were committed to their vision, and today Americans enjoy the freedom they sought.

Just as their commitment to a vision empowered these historical figures, so too can your commitment to your own vision empower you. Yes, you will face opposition, but you'll also become aware that everything you need to reach that vision will be available when you are committed. Commitment works to crystalize your vision, making it clear what you need to do and what you need to let go of. The shiny objects that sidetrack others will not distract you since they will fade away.

One day when driving to pick up the kids from school while crying on my old Google phone to my mother-in-law, she gifted an ear while I vented my frustrations. On this particular call, she reminded me to thank God for my life and to be grateful. I knew at that moment I couldn't cave into the despair of being homeless or bury how it made me feel. I needed to make the best of this situation and commit to it for the sake of my family.

It was in my commitment to search for the good in my situation, that my life changed. That shift in mindset to commit to my vision through gratitude changed my perspective, my focus, and my life.

As I began to feel empowered by my commitment, I started learning the lessons that could benefit not only my family and me, but others and maybe even my future grandchildren as well. My commitment activated my brain's ability to recognize the amazing story within our situation and the capability I had to write about it and share it with others. This excited me, and I began to find the laughter, love, and light in what I had previously considered a dark experience. I began dreaming about writing a book to teach others to learn from their stories, and I even visualized telling my story on *The Oprah Winfrey Show* or *The Ellen DeGeneres Show*. My high commitment to my vision has empowered me to assemble the team and resources needed to make this book a reality.

We Get What We Need

You have way more influence over your life than you realize. When you commit to being more loving, more love will show up. Commit to being joyful, and more joy will show up. Commit to being curious and learning from your experiences, and you'll learn a whole bunch. It feels like it would be the opposite, but it isn't. Commit to a positive change, and life will happen for you as you tap into the power to take control of your vision, your focus, your choices, and your decisions. This doesn't mean that life isn't done handing you challenges, but now you understand how to handle them in a way that enables you to decide on and take an active role in the outcome! Challenges will take up much less time and emotion since your laser-focused commitment will enable you to easily let go of what no longer serves you.

When you commit to your vision, you will find the path that leads to it, and you will find what you need along the way. You'll find yourself coming across necessary resources and situations, meeting the exact person who can help you reach the next stepping-stone and progressing step-by-step. These resources, people, and situations that come into your life are the steps that lead to your vision. You will see it coming together in a way that will reinforce your commitment and ignite your excitement. Yes, you have empowered yourself and are on the way to achieving your vision.

We all have desires, hopes, and dreams that the world will send us what we want. Wanting to save more money, spend more time with the family, or start a business are nothing more than wishes if there is no forward action, promise, or commitment that supports those desires. A real commitment is spoken like this: I will absolutely invest fifty dollars of every paycheck into my investment account for one year. Or maybe this: I am absolutely committed to a loving relationship with my spouse. Recall these visions when challenges arise. A true commitment is a promise and involves belief in yourself and faith to carry it out, which is why it can be hard for some people to commit. You need to be selective and not haphazard with the promises you make; you need to be impeccable with your word. It could be that your vision is revolutionary, like those of the historical figures we read about earlier. Whether your commitments are big or small, you may need to defend your commitments to that vision, fight for that vision, and make it a priority when it isn't convenient.

This will only prove how empowered you are because you'll be seeing your vision through and achieving it.

I said for years that I was going to write a book, but it wasn't until I declared out loud to my entrepreneurial group that I was going to write a book that it occurred. I didn't know how I was going to do it. I certainly didn't have all the ducks in a row or even know what the ducks were supposed to look like, but I knew in my heart that I had something important to say and that I couldn't ignore the nudges any longer. I stepped out in faith.

Faith is taking the first step even when you don't see the whole staircase.
~Martin Luther King Jr.

By treating your vision with integrity and commitment, you become empowered. Rather than just trying to reach your vision and hoping life doesn't get in the way, you own your vision. Announcing full accountability for achieving your vision—I am committed to________—is when the empowerment materializes, like magic. Declaring your specific commitment out loud to another human being solidifies your promise, and writing it down with an assignment of time keeps momentum for your actions. The magic is happening when you see opportunities, meet people who can help you, and experience events that can make the journey to your vision faster or simply more enjoyable. With respect to your commitment, pick someone or a group to stay accountable to. This will strengthen your empowerment as you share your stepping-stone achievements.

Since life will give you what you need when you step out and commit, what are you committed to?

RADICAL RESPONSIBILITY

When traveling the road to a vision, there will often be unexpected turns, challenging weather, and events tending to throw you off course. It will be easy to place blame and come up with excuses for why you aren't getting to where you want to go. When this happens, you need to take the full onus of responsibility for the results.

This life you have been gifted on this planet is yours, and you are the only person responsible for getting you to your vision! It's great when you find people in life who love you, care for you, and share your dreams, but it's icing on the cake, not the cake itself. Even though there will be people who walk alongside you on your journey to your vision, you are the only person who is responsible for getting you there. No one else is responsible for getting you what you want.

Prior to losing our home, my husband and I had a couple of years of marriage counseling and learned how to navigate our relationship in a healthier way. Little did we know that we were going to have such a tremendous opportunity to put that learning into practice. Even though I knew better, the stress of the loss and uncertainty tied to it caused me to struggle with the desire to blame my husband for getting us into that mess and to blame him for all my frustrations. The time was ripe for me to choose what I was committed to and take radical responsibility for my life.

After choosing to take radical responsiblity for our situation, life shifted for me. I was then able to see how I contributed to those things I had taken issue with: negative feelings, finances, and homelessness. I changed the things I could and left the things I couldn't change to the Divine. It was like drawing a line in the sand, and it felt amazing!

God, grant me the serenity
to accept the things I cannot change,
the courage to change the things I can,
and the wisdom to know the difference.
~ Reinhold Niebuhr

Taking radical responsibility for where you are in your life, right now, enables you to see where you have fallen short, where you have screwed up, where you could have done better, and where you contributed to the dysfunction or the breakdown. Taking radical responsibility is a heavy burden, and it's easier to blame others and unburden yourself of uncomfortable feelings. But placing blame doesn't make things better for you or anyone else. Instead, it takes away your power to change your circumstances. Avoiding responsibility for the results in your life is the same as throwing your power away. It's OK to screw things up. We all do it at one time or another. As I explained in chapter 7, feeling guilty awakens your need to take action to resolve it. Feeling shame, on the other hand, takes you to a place of condemnation that in no way aligns with being unmessable. I know you're becoming unmessable because you're still reading, so face what needs to change, search for improvement opportunities, and discover what you have control over. Stop thinking like a victim.

Choose to Be a Victor—Look Through the Victor Lens

When you take radical responsibility, you accept your part and keep your power over your life, your emotions, and your results. This empowering choice will lead you to become unmessable.

The opposite of a victor lens is the victim lens, and it is usually acquired early in life. As a child, we somehow learn to take responsibility for someone else's feelings, behaviors, or circumstances. If you happen to look through this victim lens regularly, you can get rid of it and exchange it for a victor lens.

Here is a list of ways to stop feeling like a victim and start viewing life from the victor's viewpoint.

1. Take responsibility for your feelings and what happens in your life.

2. Never put yourself down.

3. Stop feeling sorry for yourself, and look for the good in your life.

4. Replace painful memories with lessons learned.

5. The grass is greener where you water it.

6. Listen to other victim stories with empathy rather than competition.

7. Keep your focus on your vision for your life, not the rearview mirror.

Start thinking of yourself as a victor, a survivor, a champion, a person who can create possibilities. Begin taking radical responsibility for your choices, decisions, and feelings. When you love yourself and create boundaries that support that love, others will love you back. If you need help, work with a coach to explore your limiting beliefs and how to create new beliefs that support your overall vision. Practice gratitude, get out of your own head, and help others.

Victors Know How to Forgive

Forgiveness is the act of choosing not to bring out the arsenal of ammunition you have against someone or something. Being able to forgive is an empowering gift you give yourself. It allows you to release those internal knots you have tied in your gut but blamed on others. Instead of waiting for a person to change or apologize, choose to release that person from his or her "crime" against you. Leave all the "evidence" you have against the person in the virtual court records. Forgiveness doesn't mean we condone what another person did. We provide it to free ourselves from the bondage created by holding something (true or not) against another person. Remember, that the way you judge others is how you ultimately judge yourself. If you want to be unmessable, you need to be your biggest champion. So forgive yourself too.

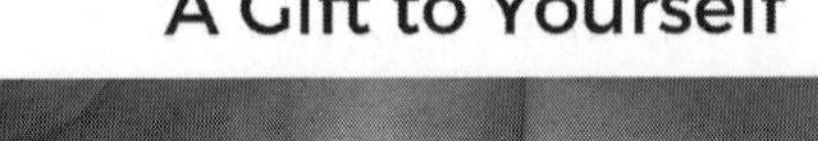

OWNING UP

When you are able to forgive, you choose to take responsibility, and this means accepting where you have fallen short and need forgiveness from others. Ask for it. It's better for you and the other person. Owning your part in any breakdown can be very liberating. It's not always easy to accept or admit when we hurt others. Forgiveness of self is often harder than forgiveness of another, but without forgiveness there can be no healing. Again, leave alone all the ammunition you have to punish yourself. Let that sh*t go, and feel the fullness of love envelop your life.

It All Leads to Empowerment

To be truly resilient in the face of all external circumstances, accept that you are fully, radically responsible for the results in your life. Only then can you accept that you have control and power to make the choices that will get you what you want. Although external circumstances and people have influence over certain life situations, ultimately all decisions belong to you. You choose how you show up, how you address things, who you choose to keep around, and what sort of behaviors you allow. You are empowered!

WHAT IS YOUR WHY?

Shifting from a victim lens to a victor lens is essential for being unmessable. It is also a process of change that may or may not take a lot of time. Some shifts require a quick change in body or language, and some shifts require getting to the bottom of a long-held belief. But each starts with a big *why*. Ask yourself the following questions to uncover why you want to take on a victor lens and become empowered and unmessable.

- Why do you want to shift?
- Why do you want to make these changes in your life?
- Why do you want to explore and challenge old ways?
- Why must you absolutely move beyond this place at this time in the world?

If you can't identify the reason why you are making this shift, then any motivation to get you through the tough times will quickly fizzle out. You have a unique reason why you want to be unmessable. To help you figure out your why, read on.

I used to blame my husband for feeling depressed, anxious, and joyless. When we separated, a counselor told him that my kids would probably learn to cope with life the same ways I had been coping if I didn't figure out how to do life differently. That knowledge became the driver for me to change. That was my why! I didn't want my kids to learn to live life with anxiety, depression, defensiveness, and blame. I had to shift! My *why* was bigger than me; other people were counting on me to shift, even if they didn't know it. Their future was riding on my changes, my shifts. I had to figure it out because I didn't want to be the person responsible for teaching them an unsustainable way to practice living. It was too painful to accept. I much more wanted to be the person who broke the pattern. Thinking I had lived knowing that I hadn't done all I could do to break dysfunctional patterns was too dreadful to allow. You need to figure out your own big why!

There will be setbacks and challenges on your journey. But you can and will reach your vision if you have a strong enough reason, a clear enough purpose, to get through the tough times staying focused and dedicated toward achieving your vision.

FOR YOUR JOURNAL

Now that you understand what it takes to become empowered, take out your journal and find a comfortable place to sit. Take a few deep breaths, spend time reading through the following questions, and take time to write down your answers with as much detail as you need.

1. After rereading the vision you created in chapter 6 of your journal, do you think of it as a commitment to that vision or as a wish? If it is a vision, take some time to decide if you are still committed to it. If not, that's OK. Take some time to figure out a vision you could commit to. Write a few sentences describing that vision with specific, clear details and a timeline.

2. Now that you have a vision you can commit to, what obstacles might challenge your commitment? List these in your journal. Then come up with a game plan ahead of time about how to address those obstacles.

3. Think about where in your life you need to increase the power of your commitment. Identify a shift that you have been trying to make without success. How have you benefitted by not making the shift or the commitment to shift?

4. What will be the cost if you choose to not stay committed to your vision? Who will suffer? Who will miss out? What negative consequences have you already experienced by not taking radical responsibility or committing?

5. Where in your life are you not taking radical responsibility? What could you lose out on as a result? What opportunities could you miss? Might your health suffer? Your love life or relationships?

6. Write as much as you need to get it all out of your head. You don't need to do anything with this; its purpose is to unburden you. Why do you think you need forgiveness? How have you hurt or hindered others? Who do you need to forgive? How is not forgiving hurting you or holding you back? After you have recorded these answers in your journal, say an internal prayer or request for guidance with your unforgiveness. Notice your feelings and thoughts, and jot them down in your journal.

7. Come up with a major reason for why you need to stay committed to your vision or make the changes you feel necessary. Write down your "why" in your journal.

CHAPTER TAKEAWAYS

1. It is through your commitments that life's external circumstances lose their power.

2. Forgiveness of yourself and others is key to empowering yourself.

3. When you take radical responsibility for your feelings, results, and outcomes, you increase your possibilities.

4. Choosing to look through a victor lens enables you to harness your personal power and become unmessable!

5. Creating a powerful *why* for reaching your vison will get you through the tough times.

Chapter 11

ANOTHER WAY TO FEEL

THIS CHAPTER IS ALL ABOUT THE WAYS in which you can always feel your best, get out of a funk, and tap into your feelings as a barometer of physical, mental, and spiritual health.

YOUR TREASURE

To feel amazing, you must know what your body needs and know that you must pay attention to what it is telling you. You owe it to yourself to treat your body as the treasure it is and to keep it in healthy condition. Learning to listen to your body and supply it with what it needs is another component to becoming unmessable. Where your health and wellness are concerned, it is wise to always take a proactive approach rather than to treat problems after they appear. The more health issues you can prevent or symptoms you can address at their earliest sign, the better off you'll be. Your body needs to be honored and respected.

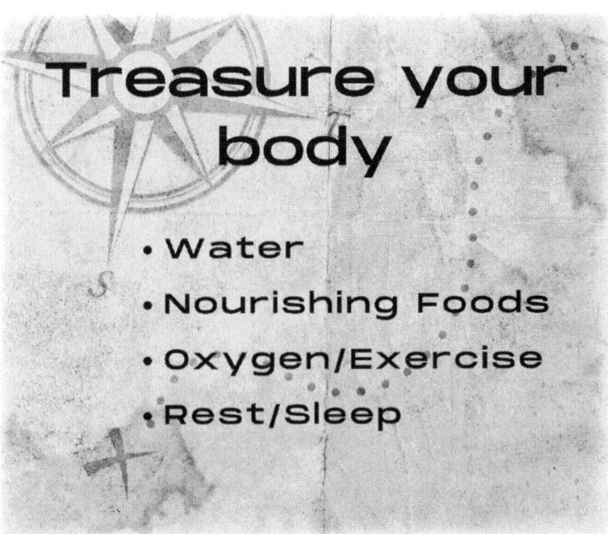

The Immune System

The immune system protects us from outside invaders, so paying special attention to what is needed to keep it healthy is beneficial and of the utmost importance. Your immune system stays strong when your body is getting what it needs—oxygen and clean air to breathe; clean water to stay hydrated; the right combination of foods to nourish and assist in growth, healing, and development; sufficient rest and relaxation to recuperate and energize; and exercise to keep the system moving so it can flush toxins from internal organs and muscles.

When you think about maximizing your immune health, you first need to consider what you are currently doing in terms of an exercise routine, diet, breathing techniques, meditation, yoga, nutrition, nutritional supplements, essential oils, and getting enough sleep. Even though they don't provide a "one size fits all" approach to health, there are general guidelines that each of us can tailor to his or her own body and to what it requires at different stages of life and throughout each day. I discovered I had more energy, less brain fog, and more joy from lower-carbohydrate eating. If you feel you aren't running at optimum efficiency, stop and figure out why. Do the necessary research and consult qualified practitioners to guide you as to what your body needs to function at its best. Then choose the approaches that fit into your lifestyle and align with the vision you have for your life. In order to be unmessable, you must decide how to best meet the needs of your body—and then do it!

MOVEMENT

How you carry yourself influences the way you think, feel, and behave. It is also an overlooked source of personal power that contributes to becoming unmessable.

Movement is more than just how you move when you walk. It's communication through body language. We communicate so much more through our bodies than we do with our words—and what's more, it truly is our actions that speak louder (and truer) than our words. Your physical form and the way you hold your body while sitting, standing, speaking in front of a group, or just generally living your life is all directly wired to your brain, and it's a two-way street. Not only do you project to others a true reflection of how you are actually feeling by how you hold your body, but you can also turn this back on yourself to influence how your body makes you feel.

The 2015 book *Presence* by Amy Cuddy analyzes 185 videos of venture capital presentations and comes to the conclusion that the biggest predictor of who would receive investments didn't depend on credentials or the content of the pitch. It was the confidence projected by the presenter. The presenter's comfort level and passionate enthusiasm was projected to potential investors through body language. What the book also found was that when people are self-focused and anxious, they are less able to relate to the people around them and, therefore, are trusted less. The presenter who projected power also projected fewer negative emotions and thereby appeared more in the moment and was trusted the most.

The same holds true for any type of social interaction. Take notice of how you hold your body when you are feeling less than powerful, even anxious, insecure, or uncertain when in the company of one person or a group. Chances are that you are holding yourself in a way that projects an aloofness. Happy, confident people radiate warmth since they appear outwardly relaxed and engaged.

When I felt depressed over our situation, I was often hunched over, with my hands on my head in disbelief and frustration. My body also displayed how scared I was as I crossed my arms in an unconscious attempt to guard or protect myself.

Movement and emotions are linked pathways in the brain. This means when we feel an emotion, such as sadness, the brain stores memories regarding the level of emotion and the way in which the body is moving or not moving at that moment, together in a pathway. Then when we feel this same emotion again, we hold our body in the same way, causing this body language to become more and more ingrained and automatic. So, even if you aren't sad but are holding your body in a particular way that is being influenced by a sad memory, you are likely to feel sad.

But you can change that!

How to Feel Powerful

Consider how you're feeling right this minute and notice how you are holding your body. Now think back to a time when you felt powerful, and relive what that felt like. You should immediately notice a natural change in your body language. Perhaps you are experiencing a grin on your face as you recall your once-felt power. Maybe your posture has changed, and you are now sitting or standing tall or unclenching your fists or raising your arms. Or maybe the change is more subtle, and your face just radiates calm.

Likewise, you can take advantage of this brain pathway and also use it in reverse. If you want to reclaim a powerful feeling from your past, consciously hold your body that same way. You will tap into that same emotion and, as a result, project that powerful feeling. Try it. Take a Wonder Woman stance or strike a victory pose in the same way people do after crossing a finish line, and plaster a huge grin on your face. Trust me. You'll feel as great as you would if you had just won a race. Physical movement holds power over emotion.

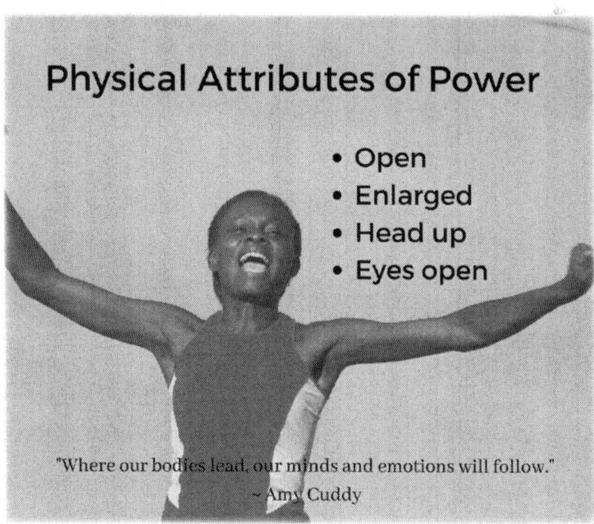

This victory pose is something easy that you can do at home, at work, on a date, before a presentation, or even in a bathroom stall before or during an event when you need to conjure up and project confidence. Teach this technique to your children or to children you know; it's a game changer. Show them that striking a victory pose before a test or a speech will put them in a better headspace and enable them to feel confident.

Joseph McLendon III is a PhD in neuropsychology and a proponent of harnessing body movement to shift into a powerful state. He recommends shaking your ass because when your ass moves, your whole body moves with it, and this movement floods your head with an invigorating brain cocktail. So when you're stressed or anxious at your workstation, at home, at school, or literally anywhere, simply wiggle your butt like you're on a dance floor and shift into a better mood.

Body movement enables you to access any emotion, negative or positive, at any time and can be used to your advantage when you align your body movements with your vision. Consciously using body movement to influence your brain's ability to access any desired emotion is yet another step toward becoming unmessable.

HITTING PAUSE

Now that you are aware of how to tap into any feeling at any time, you also need to step back, hit the pause button, and create a quiet space. That way you can focus inward for assessment of your feelings and get guidance for what is needed to put you in alignment with your vision. The ability to do this is vitally important and one of the easiest actions to take in your quest to becoming unmessable.

The reason we all need to take some time out of each day for ourselves is to keep perspective in our busy lives. Our days revolve around doing stuff. We take care of the people we love, maintain our homes, and devote time to work and play. But it's knowing how to tap into those moments in between, when all is quiet, that allows for self-reflection, and it's often when we get our best ideas, get a clear understanding of our current needs, and see a clearer way to solving problems and generating ideas about what to do next. So, whether you choose to create your quiet space while taking a shower or bath, meditating, driving, dancing, walking, or hiking, be sure to take advantage of this time to connect with yourself and just be.

I finally came to the realization while we were in the forest that I needed alone time to reflect, so Brent and the kids left me at the campsite to hang out by myself. The result was amazing. Hitting pause in my life allowed me time to focus on journaling my feelings and thoughts, like talking to a friend. This time of self-reflection also enabled me to get out of my own head and see more clearly what I had been focusing on and where I needed to shift in order to get where I wanted to go.

To be unmessable, you must be aware when your feelings are getting in the way of reaching your vision. Taking regularly scheduled pauses to reflect on your feelings and discover potential or hidden roadblocks is essential. These can be part of a daily meditation, a lunchtime reflection, or a once-a-week thought session, whatever works best for you. If you notice you've taken a detour or feel stuck, this time can help you correct your course and realign with your vision at any time.

FEELINGS CHECK

Being homeless made me feel really heavy and unable to get out of my own way. Although I tried to shift my feelings and strategize, some days I just couldn't shift my feelings, which was frustrating at the time but turned out to be a real gift. On those confusing days, I came to realize that I needed to immerse myself in my feelings—to actually listen to my feelings because they were trying to tell me something.

Feelings can convey helpful and necessary information if you allow yourself to open up to them and tune into what they are telling you.

I find the acronym HALT—short for hungry, angry, lonely, tired—gives helpful guidance to tap into what strong feelings are telling you. Knowing how to HALT shows you how to pay attention to these feelings and make a quick first assessment.

Hungry: Like the Snickers commercial says, "You're just not the same when you're hungry." If you examine your feelings and discover you're hungry, get something to eat and fuel your body and brain so they can function at optimum efficiency.

Angry: Anger is often a sign that someone has crossed a boundary. Examine your boundaries and decide how to handle any breeches or how to adjust the boundary to align with your vision.

Lonely: Loneliness is a signal that it's time to connect, so get out there and reconnect with people—and with yourself.

Tired: This one influences your entire well-being. Get enough sleep to recharge your brain and your body. Ninety-minute increments are best, but twenty-minute afternoon power naps can also be a great recharge. It is impossible to concentrate and focus on the present, not to mention the future, when you are tired.

Feelings as an Indicator of Change

Now that you have completed a quick first assessment with HALT, make any necessary adjustments. The next step is to examine any further feelings as key pieces of information in determining your current emotional well-being. For instance, you might not even be aware, but many times when you feel anxious, it's because you are thinking about the future. Anticipating the unknown can make us all feel anxious, so when that feeling comes over you, just pause and take a few breaths. This simple maneuver will work to bring you back into the present. It is in the present where you can creatively tap into the brain's ability to solve problems. Pausing also gives you the opportunity to question your anxiety by asking yourself what that anxiety is trying to tell you. It's possible your subconscious is aware that you need to prepare better or make a shift because the plans you are living your life by now will not serve you as well in the future.

As you learn to examine your feelings, you'll see that some of them are actually trying to alert you that something in your life needs attending. I wish I could tell you this could be used as a crystal ball so you could just fix things before they happened, but it's not. Being able to decode your feelings is actually listening to your gut—your intuition. These types of feelings alert you to the need for change, but it's your job to figure out what the need is and how to handle it. Your intuition is your inner guide, and it will direct you if you pause and listen.

But sometimes you just can't go it alone. In these cases it's helpful to call or text a trusted friend or confidant who can ask questions to help you decipher what's actually going on with your feelings. To be part of a safe community of people who can help you in this way is ideal, and there is one for you at our Facebook group called Be Unmessable! Community.

In the end, you need to remember that our feelings are truly and deeply personal. They are generated within us, and that makes each of us responsible for our own. It's not anyone else's responsibility to fix our feelings or constantly ask us if everything is OK. Likewise, pushing our own feelings onto someone else is also a boundary intrusion. Be careful not to cross that line or let anyone cross it in regard to your feelings.

Conviction

Faith and spiritual practice are both powerful sources that give you feelings of certainty and peace, especially in challenging times. The act of believing in something greater than yourself—a loving creator, a divine being, something with a much higher perspective—can be a great source of peace when things get tough. Whatever you believe in is welcome in this space.

I have found a great deal of comfort and peace in my belief in God and the redemption I have felt through my belief in Jesus. It was through my relationship with God, which was built over several years prior to losing everything, that I received the faith that I was going to be OK, and it gave me the strength to carry on. I trusted that my higher power had a bird's eye view of what was to come in my life and was working on my behalf, far ahead of me on the path. This trust and belief brought me great comfort when things were falling apart and the future seemed bleak.

Having a regular spiritual practice in place to assist in dealing with life's challenges makes it much easier to shift your feelings and your focus.

FOR YOUR JOURNAL

You have another key to being unmessable and for getting what you want no matter what life throws at you. Now that you understand how you can shift your feelings, it's time to put this knowledge into practice. Take out your journal and find a comfortable place to sit. Take a few deep breaths, spend some time reading through the following questions, and write down your answers in as much detail as you need.

1. Tune into how your body feels. Starting at your toes, go to your feet, to your legs, and then all the way up to your head. Take a body inventory with particular attention to how you feel in general. Do any parts of your body signal a health need? If so, which ones need attention? List them.

2. Make a list of ten possible ways you can strengthen your immune system and its influence in addressing and healing any of your bodily needs.

3. Put down your pen and stand up. Now practice the victory pose while smiling, jumping up and down, and shaking your ass. Record how these movements change how you feel. Figure out which five movements most easily shift your feelings to a positive place. Note them in your journal so that you remember and are prepared in advance for when you need them to combat a feeling that you are challenged by or at a low time. Make a list of these five as the ways you enjoy moving your body that also serve to shift your feelings when necessary, and practice them daily.

4. Use your phone to schedule two reminders, one in the morning and one in the afternoon, to pause and do a feelings check. Follow that

with the necessary course corrections to stay aligned with your vision.

5. Use your calendar to schedule time every week to pause and take a hike or simply walk, dance, bicycle, or undertake any other physical activity that disconnects you from the busy doing of life and allows you to just *be*. Take notice of any thoughts that occur during this time and make notes in your journal about them—notes that might help you in your current or future life.

6. Journal your regularly occurring feelings and what they are telling you about yourself. What are you learning from them? Take particular notice of how certain specific feelings relate to your particular needs.

CHAPTER TAKEAWAYS

1. Protect your body's immune system proactively through proper health, including healthful eating, drinking, exercising, and sleeping habits.

2. Use body movement to shift how you feel by making the victory pose, dancing, shaking your ass, or making up some movements of your own.

3. Take regular pauses for a feelings check so as to align those feelings with your vision and to implement any course correction needed.

4. Immerse yourself in strong feelings (do not avoid them) so that you can tap into the power that will tell you what you truly need.

5. Believe in a power greater than yourself as a source of comfort and peace in times of challenge.

Chapter 12

ANOTHER WAY TO LIVE

THIS CHAPTER WILL SHOW YOU HOW to change your world and how to effect necessary change in the world around you. In this way, you can consciously choose the framework for your life and fulfill your purpose all while becoming unmessable.

Often when life throws us challenges, we spend so much time either being upset by the challenges or complaining that we don't deal with them at all. What these two reactions have in common is that they leave us stuck in confusion and feeling anxious because challenging what we know means that things are changing, and we don't know what the future will bring. What seemed secure is now up for grabs. Both are also normal reactions that most of us go through when faced with an unexpected challenge. In fact, we may even experience both reactions at different times in our lives or even simultaneously as we try to cope with a single challenge. But while we're busy reacting, we miss out on the fact that actually most challenges are gifts in disguise, and the faster we can accept a challenge as a gift, the faster we can get to solving the dilemma it presents or come to an understanding of its true purpose.

ACCEPTANCE

Let's begin by understanding how to accept a challenge, which means you first need to come up with a way to speak to yourself about it. Think of it as a brainstorming session with yourself. Speaking with yourself about a challenge enables you to get it all out of your head and to look at it through a neutral lens, allowing you to come up with more possible solutions or ways to deal with it.

There are many ways to speak with yourself about a challenge. My way is to pray out loud in my car and journal on my computer. Feel free to adopt my way, or perhaps you may prefer to take voice notes, meditate, create art, or come up with something completely unique. At any rate, the point is to address the challenge and not avoid it. This is not a time to bury your head in the sand. By facing a challenge head on, you rob it of its power over your automatic brain. (When you describe the challenge to yourself, you are going to listen in a neutral way, like a reporter. See chapter 9 for a refresher on my suggestions for neutral listening.) Begin the talking or writing by stating the facts. State what the challenge is—exactly. Do not add emotion or embellish your story; just supply the facts. You may find that you have more than one challenge to deal with, and this is normal, as challenges are seldom simple or straightforward. Think of a tree. The trunk is the like the base challenge, but there are many branches that sprout out of the base. These may be consequences of the main challenge or offshoots of the main challenge. List them all, and treat them as separate challenges. This is because a challenge is multifaceted, and there is never one solution or lesson. Some of these challenges might be bigger than others, but they all need to be dealt with on their own even though they are connected. Separate the issues.

Next, ask yourself the following questions or similar ones that align more closely with your vision:

- What can I learn from this challenge?
- What is great about this challenge, or how could this be a gift in disguise?
- How can I adapt to this challenge and stay in alignment with my vision?
- What possibilities is this challenge creating for me?
- What is my immediate gut reaction from my inner guide/intuition/Holy Spirit? These are the answers your gut comes up with right away. Write them down or record them as a reminder on your phone.

These questions will give you what you need to finally take action, either big or small, that will help you begin to unravel the challenge you are facing. These questions help you sort out the possibilities that arose from your acceptance process and willingness to take charge. Taking this first action toward your vision will get you started. Your next step is to stay in touch and focused, using your intuition and vision to lead you to taking the next step. It will reveal itself to you as you examine every aspect of the challenge facing you. Taking both the small and big actions necessary to navigate around the obstacles that this challenge has put in your way will lead you to your destination/vision.

STEP INTO THE LIGHT

One thing you need to remember is that your story is a unique story, and only you can tell it. The world wants to hear from you. Even if your information doesn't seem different from what others have to say, it's your perspective that sets you apart. Step into the light! Don't deny the world from hearing your story.

In my own personal development journey, I found that my purpose was to create the possibility for women everywhere, of every background, to *all* become unmessable and who they were created to be. But it took time to figure it out. In my earlier days, I spent a great deal of time trying to be someone I wasn't, to fit in, to get people to like and approve of me. I would avoid speaking my mind or giving my opinions for fear that they would drive people away. I would accept behavior that I did not agree with from others so that I didn't offend or break connection. That proved to be a tiring and fruitless effort. Pretending to be someone you are not is an act of deception that takes a toll on your soul. It is exhausting and impossible to maintain, especially when you need to keep up the facade to stay in any type of relationship. For in the end it all comes down to this: If people don't like you for who you really are, then they aren't part of your crowd, your community, your circle.

The best person you can be is the one who is true and fully yourself.

Today you are you, that is truer than true. There is no one alive who is you-er than you. Shout aloud, I am glad to be what I am. Thank goodness I'm not a ham, or a clam, or a dusty old jar of gooseberry jam. I am what I am, what a great thing to be. If I say so myself, happy everyday to me! ~ Dr. Seuss

---

Today Oprah Winfrey is ranked as the most influential woman in the world, but in her early career she was a news co-anchor who got fired because she was unable to separate her emotions from her stories. But Oprah used what others thought as a failing to create "The Oprah Winfrey Show," the highest-rated television program of its kind in the history of television. She is a self-made multibillionaire and one of the greatest philanthropists in American history. Imagine what the world would have missed out on if Oprah had shrunk back because of someone's opinion about how she expressed her emotions. Daytime television was changed forever, and she made feeling authentic acceptable both for herself and for the rest of us. She had the courage to give us the gift of her true self.

Likewise, in the early days of her career, Alecia Moore, aka singer-songwriter Pink, was compared by the tabloids to Britney Spears and Christina Aguilera and encouraged to be more like them to increase her popularity. Today Pink is one of music's most successful stars, having sold more than forty-two million albums. In August 2019, the Beautiful Trauma World Tour, the biggest of her career, became the highest-grossing tour by a woman in this decade, according to Billboard Boxscore. She headlines arenas and inspires women and girls throughout the world to be themselves and is one of my all-time favorite performers. Imagine if she had listened to others and not been true to herself. We would all have missed out on getting to enjoy the music that only she can bring to the world.

When people reject you—and they will—so what? Rather than worry about what other people think or say about you, instead I want you to be unmessable and make a game of it by separating out who isn't in your crowd from who is. When someone criticizes you for your choices, make a mental note: *not one of my people.* The point is to enjoy the weeding out process and the disapproval of the people who aren't your crowd, your fans, your circle—those who don't approve of the real you. Live as yourself in full force and filter out those people. After all, you don't really need them in your life. Thanks to the internet, you can choose from the 7.6 billion people on the planet and find the people who align with your vision for your life. In this case your challenge is the crowd; face it straight on! (Refer back to chapter 9 and get some coaching on how not to take things personally, if that makes your life easier.)

I leave you to ponder this truism: Often, when people criticize, it says so much more about them than the one they are criticizing. If you are the object of their criticism, take nothing personally. It might be hard, but if you practice, it will become second nature. In my experience, it's those who are uncomfortable with you being all of who you are who criticize in an attempt to get you to shrink back and align with their way of thinking so that they can feel OK about themselves. Think of these people as needing to make you wrong so that they can feel right. Many people aren't OK with feeling wrong, so they have to come up with ways to make you wrong so that they don't have to feel the feelings that go along with being wrong. They don't currently have the personal skills or self-love that allows them to let you be you, and that's OK. They're not your people right now.

Don't hide your true self and play the small game. Instead, show yourself in the light, play full on, live large! The world needs you, your unique perspective, and the story only you can tell.

Neither do people light a lamp and put it under a bowl. Instead they put it on its stand, and it gives light to everyone in the house. Matthew 5:15

Avoid being one of those who wonders what one person can do to change the world when there is so much that needs to be changed. One person can do quite a lot just by becoming self-aware and allowing his or her true personality to show through, as you are now doing. Strive for your next level up and influence the people around you in a visible, positive way. The ripple of your change will cause others to change in more ways than you can count.

Up until now this book has been building a case to prove to you that you have within yourself the ability to choose and succeed at becoming who you desire to be. Chapter 9, on listening, gave you insights on improving your listening so that you can better tune into your inner, intuitive guiding voice. I'm betting that voice has now become louder, and you are now hearing what you weren't able to clearly hear before: You aren't living up to all of who you are, you're holding back in close relationships, you're holding back your voice at work, or you're holding back a piece of you with your friends. Listen, listen, listen to that inner voice, and do what you can to turn up the volume and never hold yourself back. Chances are, you've heard enough whispers from this voice in the past. You just didn't know what it was or how to tune into it while it alerted you to the fact that you weren't playing full-on or being all of who you were created to be. Listen to your inner voice. The world needs you to show your unique self now!

"Our deepest fear is not that we are inadequate. Our deepest fear i s that we are powerful beyond measure. It is our light, not our darkness that most frightens us. We ask ourselves, 'Who am I to be brilliant, gorgeous, talented, fabulous?' Actually, who are you not to be? You are a child of God. Your playing small does not serve the world. There is nothing enlightened about shrinking so that other people won't feel insecure around you. We are all meant to shine, as children do. We were born to make manifest the glory of God that is within us. It's not just in some of us; it's in everyone. And as we let our own light shine, we unconsciously give other people permission to do the same. As we are liberated from our own fear, our presence automatically liberates others." ~Marianne Williamson, A Return to Love: Reflections on the Principles of "A Course in Miracles"

Playing full-on means changing up how you navigate this life so that you are free to live another way!

CHOOSE YOUR PARADIGM WISELY

Many people on this earth live life through a common paradigm we've learned to adapt to and go along with. It is the paradigm of *do, have, be.* I first heard about this concept at a Generative Solutions training seminar in Austin, Texas.

We get caught up in our daily lives of staying busy doing things so that we can have what we want. But we're so busy that we forget to choose who we want to be or need to be to reach our actual vision. You wake up in the morning and think about what clothes you're going to wear to work, what has to be done to get the kids to school, what tasks need to get completed for your business clients, and what errands you need to finish during your day before it all starts again the next morning.

Many of us are brought up to believe the answer to what is wrong in life can be fixed if we have more of certain things (money, time, certain clothes, a particular car, a bigger house, confidence). It's as if having these things is a requirement to do what we want (like starting a business, changing jobs, going on vacation, buying a house, finding a life partner), which in turn allows us to "be" what we want (valuable, stable, happy, confident, content, less anxious, not so angry). We are a society of very busy doers, and as an entrepreneur, I know that nothing happens without an action to make it happen. But often we get so busy doing and miss out on some of the essential actions needed to be unmessable. These essential ways of being enable us to really take advantage of living this one short life that we have to the fullest!

What Are You Doing?

This paradigm makes us think we need to *do* things in order to *have* things so that we can *be* someone. Advertisers love when we live by this paradigm and do their best to encourage us to keep doing it because it makes them billions of dollars. When we brush our teeth (*do*) with their product, we will *have* super-white teeth, and then we will *be* superspecial because we will look as good as our favorite celebrity. We are constantly bombarded with this type of advertising. It becomes part of what motivates us (like it or not) to make certain purchases, ranging from whitening toothpaste to luxury cars and homes and everything in between. For instance, when your friend only gets her hair cut by some special stylist at such and such salon, chances are she is living this paradigm. She might be thinking unconsciously that a haircut from this one stylist has the power to create a hairstyle great enough to generate lots of compliments, which means she is beautiful. Now this doesn't mean you can't get your hair cut by your own special stylist. There's nothing wrong with that. It's about how you perceive it. For example, what happens if the special hairstylist quits cutting hair or doesn't land the specific haircut you envisioned. Does that mean that you will no longer be beautiful, desirable, or valuable? No! No! No! It doesn't. You were beautiful, desirable, and valuable before you went there.

The *do-have-be* paradigm is the perfect setup for disappointment and unnecessary suffering. Living by this paradigm is what keeps people spinning their wheels with anxiety, suffering from depression, and making endless to-do lists. However, when you're not tied to *this* paradigm—which keeps you controlled by means of outside circumstances, events, and opinions—you get to choose the paradigm by which you prefer to live your life so you can be sure it lines up with your vision. This is free will.

Be You!

The ability to switch up your paradigm and flip the order to *be, do, have* is key to becoming unmessable. This paradigm starts with who you are, and it has the power to shift your life dramatically.

Start this process by declaring who you want to be and who you need to be to reach your vision.

We started with vision in chapter 6 because it's so important to be clear about your vision for the future, where you want to end up. If you are clear on what is your vision, then it's time to ask yourself if who you are being now is what is needed to get you to your vision.

Who Am I?

We are human beings, not human doings. ~ Dalai Lama

It's possible that how you choose to express yourself in life on a daily basis isn't how you need to express yourself in order to reach your vision. This doesn't mean that you need to be someone who you are not. In fact, the opposite is true. It means that you need to examine how you are expressing yourself to the world, how you are being, and examine whether or not you are expressing a true image of who you are inside. Hold your current persona up to your vision. Is your way of being, how you express yourself, in alignment with your vision for your life? For instance, if you want a life of adventure and variety, if you present yourself to others and to situations in life expressing timidity and hesitation, you are not going to get to your vision anytime quickly. Examine who you are being and make any necessary adjustments. Again, if your vision is a life of adventure and variety and you start by being courageous or spontaneous, rather than timid or hesitant, how might your approach to making the changes needed to reach your vision change? Imagine what difference any change would make in the way you do things and how those changes could result in helping or hindering getting what you envision.

I'm sure you've heard this before, or you may have even said it yourself: "If I could just make more money, then I could buy a house, and then I'd be content." Now consider the flip of it: "I am content, and in my calm contentment, I will find a lender who will give me a mortgage with no money down and I will have a new house." The second is the ideal place to come from because it begins with what you really want, to be content, but you don't have to do things or have things in order to be content. The same goes for any ways of being. Try these ways of being on for size: I am loving, I am confident, I am beautiful, I am connected, I am present, I am fabulous, I am abundant, I am free to choose, I am open, I am courageous, I am inspiring, I am flexible, and I am healthy. All your dos and haves need to first emerge from who you are.

When we were homeless, I was totally focused on wanting a house and feeling anxious about not having one. I believed that having a house would make me feel content. That thought caused me to spend a great deal of time busying myself doing things that I thought would get me into a house. I browsed craigslist rentals, drove through neighborhoods in search of For Rent signs, and engaged in hours of conversation with my husband, but the one thing I didn't do was focus on who I was or how I was being. Because I was coming from a place of scarcity, in my mind I thought of myself as poor, broke, and unwanted. This was not an ideal starting point. The shift came for me once I was able to feel content without having the house. By first being grateful for where I was, reminding myself that I was abundant, then doing things while feeling content and grateful and abundant, I knew that I already had what I dearly wanted and that having a house had nothing to do with it. What a surprise to be able to claim those positive feelings that were already part of me—the me without the house! But I did have a home, and I began to thank God for that home, a campsite with a thin orange nylon tent from Walmart. It wasn't a house, but it was our home for the time being and where we made a life together as a loving and caring family. When we finally did move into a house, of course I was excited, but by then there was not so much emotional weight attached to having it, which was fortunate because a few weeks after moving in we had to leave because of the mold issue.

What I discovered was that when I started expressing gratitude for what I had, I was able to free my mind to think of what I could do with what I had, and that led me to achieving what I wanted to have. This worked because my thoughts were coming from a place of calm and gratitude rather than scarcity and anxiety. This enabled me to open up my mind and be confident enough to imagine new possibilities for ways to accomplish getting what I wanted.

My energy was stronger coming from a place of contentment and gratitude rather than from the dark hole of desperation. My new, optimistic outlook worked to create a new pathway in my brain that brought about an even greater abundance of ideas.

This shift is super significant and helps you get what you really want in life. Once you know who you are inside and become committed to fully showing up in a way that's in alignment with your true self and your vision, you'll be surprised how this shift in your state of mind works to change so many other things in your life. You'll be wonderfully surprised, as I was, by how many things seemed to clear up with less effort than I could have ever imagined possible.

I like to use the example about the Declaration of Independence that I heard from Elizabeth Byrd at a Generative Solutions training seminar. When the country's first settlers arrived here from England and declared who they were (*be*)—which was courageous freedom fighters declaring independence from England—they had to back up those words by fighting (*do*), and in order to defend that declaration, they claimed (*have*) America, a free country to call their own. These courageous individuals started by committing to their vision of freedom and were able to truly see and believe in themselves, do the work, take a stand, and create a brand-new country. I'd say that's the ultimate shift!

Take a lesson from our country's founders, who knew their personal value did not come from what they had or what they did. Your personal value comes from knowing that you are truly valuable just as you are. Use that knowledge to get to where you want, to achieve your vision. Listen to that little voice inside telling you who you really are! Disregard that other voice that tries to protect you from the haters who will judge you. Listen for that soft inner voice that is always there if you'd only listen because it can reinforce your desires—the ones you have been ignoring. Listen, and you will know for certain what you were meant to do in this world, the reason you're here. Nurture that knowledge as you would a little baby. Give it nourishment, attention, and love, and you will be rewarded with a fulfilling life.

INTO-ME-SEE: FINDING YOUR PEOPLE

As you practice being unmessable by living another way, you'll need to be part of a safe community of people who will support you while you practice and move toward your vision for your life. You need to find your people! At first, you'll probably feel vulnerable sharing your thoughts and desires with others, but don't let that stop you from sharing. Long ago a counselor by the name of Tracy Wright shared with me that intimacy can best be described as, *into-me-see*. It means that when you let people in and they get to see the real you, you are, in effect, letting them inside you, which is very intimate and why you feel vulnerable. The good news is that this is all OK. In fact, it's an amazing feeling when you open up to someone and then feel fully accepted as you are! The takeaway is to search out a person or a group of people who can show you empathy when you express your experiences of shame, which will give you the opportunity to build up your shame resilience.

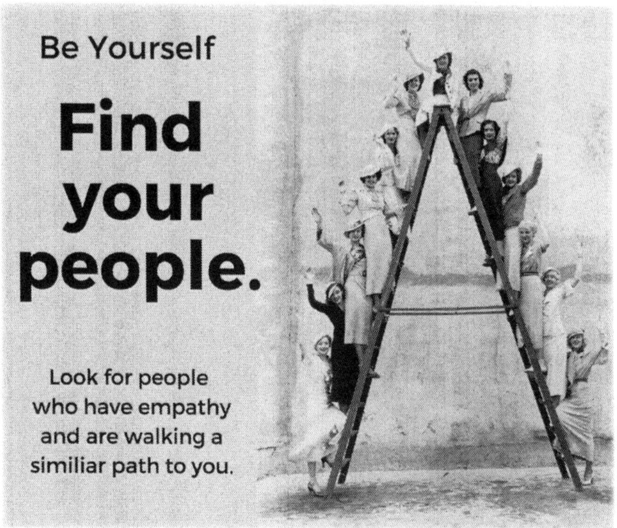

Nowadays there are so many opportunities to find like-minded people and join groups that gather and meet online to practice and do life together. Through the magic of the internet, you can develop amazing, long-lasting friendships and mentorships with people from all over the world.

Find your like-minded people, who will be there to support you on your journey of learning to be all of who you are! When you poke your head out of your shell and begin to show the world who you really are, it's common to experience some pushback, so it's essential to practice your new way of living with those who encourage you, pick you up when you stumble, and cheer you as you learn to fully express your true self!

To experience all of this and much more, join our private Facebook group called Be Unmessable! Community.

MAKING YOUR CONTRIBUTION

I'm very certain that you are a person who wants to use your time in this world to make an impact. Because you feel this way, don't forget to consciously commit to making your human need of contribution a priority. Through giving of ourselves by way of our time and talent (or money), we fulfill that need to feel purpose and spirituality in life.

By contributing in any way we can to people or causes in our communities and societies, this simple act serves to do the following:

- Fill us like nothing else
- Get us out of our heads and into our hearts
- Instill in us an amazing feeling
- Give meaning to living

When you find a way to contribute or add value to another person's life, it changes you for the better. It will fulfill you like nothing else ever has and give your life added purpose and meaning. Search for any opportunity to contribute, and one will appear. I can't say this enough: You have a lot to share, so share it! You have knowledge, time, and experiences that other people can learn from, so share them! Share yourself to serve others!

Our prime purpose in this life is to help others. And if you can't help them, at least don't hurt them. ~Dalai Lama

---

SHOWING GRATITUDE

If there is one practice that has made the most difference in my life, it's showing gratitude. We humans often complain about what we don't have. We're wired that way. But we would be better served if instead we consciously chose to be more aware of what we do have, especially if we desire to live another way. Showing gratitude is an easy way to assess the abundance in your life. God has blessed you and me with so much. Look for it, choose to see it, choose to acknowledge it, be grateful for it, and so much more will come to you.

Make it a daily practice upon awakening and before bed to think of five things you are grateful for in your life. The longer you do this, the easier it becomes to recognize the things you have to be grateful for and the more abundance you will reap in your life. Be grateful in every circumstance.

LOVE OTHERS

Love is what life is all about. Being able to give unconditional love makes an immeasurably positive impact on another human, and we all have that power. When your doing comes by way of love, life will shift for you!

Do everything in love. ~Corinthians 16:14

An act of loving can be as simple as smiling, saying a kind word, or getting involved—sharing your valuable time. Encourage conversation by asking others about themselves and by being fully present by listening to what they say. Don't get caught up in your own head, thinking and analyzing. People will be able to feel your absent energy. Instead, be selfless and focus on the those around you and what's important to them, what they need, and what and how you can contribute. You never truly know what someone is going through unless you ask. We were the family at the Flagstaff Library hanging out for hours when the afternoon rains raged outside. No one knew that I was worried whether people could tell that we were homeless.

Show vulnerability first. When you have something in common or can relate to someone's situation, open up, offer your story, and invite that person to see inside your heart. Invite both the people who are like you and those who aren't. Be curious and lean into conversations to allow you to understand other people and their perspectives.

Spend time with others and offer your presence fully by putting away your phone, turning off the TV, and giving the real gift of listening and offering empathy through heartfelt conversation.

Show you love yourself by taking good care of your body, spirit, and mind. Schedule time for yourself in nature—alone time for journaling, meditating, and listening to your divine guidance. Pour into yourself the time and energy to transform yourself into all you were created to be.

Step out in faith and choose to believe the best about people, including your neighbors and the other inhabitants of our world. Question your existing opinions and perspectives about the world and about love. Don't fall into the trap of telling yourself that people don't care. Do this and you encourage your brain to look for the evidence that backs up that belief. Instead, look for the love that is all around you. It may show up in surprising ways you aren't even aware of. It might even be your spouse nagging you to take care of yourself because of a desire to want you around for a long time to come. Or it might be a parent offering unsolicited advice, reflecting an opinion based on different experience. Or it might be your teenage kids pushing back against your discipline or advice because you're safe to push back against. They might be testing the limits to becoming all of who they are. Look for the love, the good, and the wonderful in all you do!

We need to love people even when they're awful. I'm not talking about condoning bad behavior or keeping toxic people in your life. I'm talking about offering love even to those who are not showing it themselves. Set boundaries to guard your heart and mind and don't be afraid to uphold those boundaries. But what I mean by loving people even when they are awful is committing yourself to loving people just as they are, being curious and understanding and not negative or judgmental. Being able to love yourself and others includes acknowledging that we all have a light and a dark side. Loving others in spite of those two sides means understanding and accepting that everyone can have either good or bad actions at times, and when a person shows his or her dark side, it doesn't make that person a bad person. Loving means we ask others to change bad behavior, but our love is not conditioned on those others being perfect or without flaws.

Choose to care about those who choose to be around you. There are many people who care about you, so look for them and be open when you find them. They are likely all around you! Think about everyone you know: They could be close or casual and may include church friends, family members, people you work with, and neighbors. Don't get picky about wanting to only have love from one particular person in your life. Mix it up, and enjoy receiving the love from all the people around you. And be open to meeting people and making new friends.

We all need and want to receive love, but remember that love goes both ways. So check in with yourself periodically to see if you are showing love for the people in your life. Chances are if you are longing for compliments, others are too, so give them out when you can. If you are longing for quality time with friends, be present for them too.

Do the best you can until you know better. Then when you know better, do better. ~Maya Angelou

---

I leave you now trusting that I have equipped you with the keys to live another way and to be unmessable, no matter the circumstance. You now know—and cannot deny—that you have the power within yourself to make the necessary changes to play full-on and be true to yourself.

It's up to you to decide whether or not you commit to being fully you!

FOR YOUR JOURNAL

Take out your journal and find a comfortable place to sit. Take a few deep breaths, and spend some time reading through the following questions. Then take all the time you need to write down your answers in as much detail as you feel necessary.

1. Choose a day

    a. Make a list of everything you do during that one day—all twenty-four hours—one item per line.

    b. Take your completed list and note next to each *do* item what was the resulting *have*. Examine your results.

    Example: (*do*) Clean up kitchen = (*have*) result is less clutter and less anxiety.

    - (*do*) Conversation with husband about feelings = (*have*) result is feelings of closeness and being understood.

    c. Choose any three events you'd like to do over (if you had a magic wand) and modify them by writing down what you would have liked the result to have been if you could have done it again. Go through the three events again, and this time choose who you would have to be, show up, or how you would have to express yourself and be, to get the result you really want (the do-over result you wrote down).

2. In your journal, address the following:

a. List ten things that are easy to love about yourself.

b. List five things that are not easy to love about yourself.

c. Review the list of things you love about yourself, and read each one out loud, and as you do, remember to fill yourself with the feelings of gratitude.

d. Go through the list of things not easy to love about yourself, and forgive yourself for each one. If it's part of your spiritual practice, ask God for forgiveness.

e. Go through the list of things not easy to love about yourself again, and for each item say, "I love you _____(name), and I accept that you have ______(difficult item). You are human and perfectly imperfect."

f. Journal about any items you feel you need to look into with more depth. Address those items with a coach or an accountability partner.

3. Make a list of ten ways to contribute more to your family, your people, your community, and your world. Implement one contribution each week for the next ten weeks. Continue to come up with ways to contribute to your world each week, and journal about your experiences of putting them into practice.

4. Every morning and evening list five things you are grateful for. Keep these lists in a separate gratitude journal, or list them on social media and share them with the world. See how many days in a row you can

come up with the entire five! At the end of the week, record in your journal what you've felt or experienced when focusing on gratitude each day of the week.

5. Start each morning with a vision of who you need to be in order to get what you really want out of that day. At the end of the day, see how you did and what you want to adjust. Write it in your journal.

    - Example: I want to have a great day; I need to be loving and joyful. I want to sell three courses today; I need to be outgoing, confident, persistent, and knowledgeable.

CHAPTER TAKEAWAYS

1. Choose your paradigm intentionally: *be, do, have*

2. The best person you can be is fully yourself. Learn about yourself, and love yourself unconditionally—the light and the dark.

3. Contribution feels amazing, and it gives life purpose and fulfillment.

4. Gratitude is the best and easiest way to focus on your abundance, which brings more abundance.

5. Practice doing by using love as a starting point.

Chapter 13

WRAPPING IT UP

EACH OF THE PRECEDING CHAPTERS in Part II Live Another Way led to a simple process for facing any of life's dramas and challenges. You can find this one-page process below and as a printable pdf on karenpohlman.com/unmessableprocess so that you can print it out and post it in your car, kitchen, or office or carry it in your purse.

FACING LIFE'S CHALLENGES

In the table below, you'll find the unmessable process for facing any challenge. The column on the left will list each key area of being unmessable, and the column on the right is a place for you to fill in your findings from all your journal work throughout the book.

As an example, the column on the left, under Another Way to Think, says, "Help your brain get off autopilot to support great decision-making and to get to acceptance and opportunity faster."

unmessable

Live Another Way	Your Unique Process
Another Way to Think Help your brain get off autopilot, to support great decision-making and to get to acceptance and opportunity faster.	**Another Way to Think**
Another Way to See Recall your vision for what you are truly aiming for in life overall and in whatever category your challenge is related to. Keep focused on your vision. Choose to consider other perspectives.	**Another Way to See**
Another Way to Communicate Speak out what the challenge is, in a neutral way. Ask questions that align with your vision. Be supportive and build yourself up with your language.	**Another Way to Communicate**
Another Way to Listen Listen for what your intuition is saying to you. Listen for divine or spiritual guidance.	**Another Way to Listen**
Another Way to Empower Recommit to your overall vision. Take 100% responsibility for your situation. Blame no one.	**Another Way to Empower**
Another Way to Feel Notice and adjust your body to best support your vision. Put your body in an empowered state.	**Another Way to Feel**
Another Way to Live Focus first on who you need to be to best face this challenge. Lean on your crowd for support. Continue to practice your unmessable strategies. Contribute	**Another Way to Live**

In the column on the right, use your notes from your journaling to come up with your own personal way that you will implement this strategy. Your entry may say something like this: deep breathing technique, stay relaxed, and speak out my situation to my voice recorder on the phone like a reporter.

Go through each of the strategies on the unmessable process sheet, looking back to your notes from your journaling, and come up with ways that you will implement each of the strategies to create your own personal process for being unmessable—no matter what life throws at you.

KEY TAKEAWAYS FROM THE BOOK

1. Use your personalized unmessable process from chapter 13 whenever you experience a challenge. Let it be your personal guide for getting through anything while staying true to yourself and your vision
2. Make noticing and learning about yourself a lifelong journey
3. Love yourself unconditionally—all of you. Perfection is not a real thing; strive for excellence. You are responsible for you!
4. Build yourself and others up on a daily basis. Remind yourself daily why you are choosing to live another way.
5. Consider that the thoughts you easily go to may not be accurate. Get curious and open up to other possibilities.
6. Be patient. You are learning a new way.
7. Get out of your own head, and focus on what other people need. Love everyone!
8. Reach out to other people who are on a similar path. It's always great to have an understanding ear.

9. Ask for help! Adopt the belief that there are no dumb questions.

In order to become unmessable, you need to practice on a daily basis. You need to stay in community with people who understand how this works and who will walk alongside you, encouraging your journey of growth while you practice and get stronger.

My challenge to you is to join our Facebook group, Be Unmessable! Community, and continue your growth by joining the next online book study to be unmessable at https://tinyurl.com/unmessablebookstudy.

Thank you for listening to my story and perspectives and for being open to the possibilities they can bring to your time here on earth. I look forward to seeing you in one of our book studies and keeping in touch through our online groups.

All the best!

Karen
xo

Acknowledgments

LIFE HAS INTRODUCED ME TO countless people who have helped me to discover more of who I was created to be, and for that I am truly grateful. The personal development path has brought me to seminars, books, counselors, conferences, support groups, church ministries, and business groups, and it has allowed me to mentor women from all walks of life. It has been a tremendous gift. I am grateful that there are people like you, the reader, who have that inner knowing that there is more to life than maybe what you've experienced so far. I believe God brings the people we need into our life at the exact right time, and it's up to each of us to figure out what we're supposed to be gleaning from these relationships. There are a whole bunch of people who have walked alongside me during my journey, and I wouldn't be where I am today without them. I am filled with gratitude.

First, thank-you goes to God, who has given me grace, guided me for my highest good and the highest good of everyone concerned, loved me, and chosen me. I feel endlessly loved and grateful.

This book would not have happened without the support of my husband, Brent, my biggest cheerleader, my biggest challenge (LOL!). You are my love, my friend, my business partner, my companion and my soul mate. I'm grateful we figured our sh*t out. You are a gift! You inspired me to become unmessable. Thanks for all the pushes and for believing in me. I love you always!

Thanks to my children: Jade, Cole, and Amethyst. You are my three gems; I love you always and forever and am so proud of the people you have grown up to become. You have inspired me to be a better human. You were what kept me going during our most challenging times. Thank you for believing in me and this work and encouraging me to keep going.

Thank you to my family of origin: Kathy and Brian (Mom and Dad), and my sisters, Julie and Diane. Thank you for loving me unconditionally, encouraging and believing in me and for providing financial and emotional support, laughs, hugs, and an endless amount of ridiculous humor, including stories that reflect "you just can't make this sh*t up!" Thanks mom, for inspiring me to be a compassionate human, and to look at things from other people's perspectives.

Thank you to my other family: the Pohlmans, the Burleys, the Kregers, and the Dulskis, all of whom have been supportive to our family along our journey. Thanks for loving us through the worst, as well as, the best of times. Thanks for your kind words, spiritual reminders, financial help, serving as an ear to vent to when times were tough, the laughs, the hugs, and the unconditional love.

Thank you to Lara Larson, who introduced me to a relationship with the Divine. You were a rare gem! I still feel your presence grounding me today. Thank you for your kindness, compassion, gentleness and grace.

Many people have been a huge support to me during my personal transformation journey. For what seemed like endless calls on the phone for support, girls' nights out and to whom I am eternally grateful; I thank Edna M, Chris G, Beth R, Tracy W, Ruth M, Emman C, Melissa R, Cyndi M, Elizabeth B, Betty S, and Brenda G.

For helping me to take what I learned and make it into a business, I thank Morna Haist and Kim Carpenter.

Included in my gratitude are the participants of numerous groups that helped me to grow and be myself: Authentic to the Core, Core 4, Generative

Solutions, Life Design Lab, The Alliance, The Circle, Revolutionary Women Global, and World Changing Women. I couldn't have completed this work without all of you!

Writing a book isn't just a one-person process, many people came together to enable this work to make it to the world. Daron Mueller, thank you for taking the time to read my manuscript and refer me to Kirsten. PJ Dempsey, thank you so much for helping me organize my words with your edits. Tom Locke, thank you for the fire hose of comments for me to consider before printing and, for the record, if they don't like the swearing, you told me so. Laura Duffy, thank you for your book cover and graphic design. Victoria Wolf, thank you for bringing my essence and style to the design of the book and my website. K.B. Jensen, thank you for helping me get this baby across the finish line.

Selected Bibliography

Brown, Brené. *Daring Greatly: How the Courage to Be Vulnerable Transforms the Way We Live, Love, Parent, and Lead.* New York: Penguin Random House Audio Publishing Group, 2017.

Brown, Brené. *The Gifts of Imperfection: Let Go of Who You Think You're Supposed to Be and Embrace Who You Are.* Center City, MN: Hazelden Publishing, 2010.

Byrd, Elizabeth, and Lawrence Edwards. "Emergence." *Generative Solutions, LLC.* Lectures presented at the Emergence Training Austin, Texas 2016

Chopra, Deepak, and Rudolph E. Tanzi. *Super Brain: Unleashing the Explosive Power of Your Mind to Maximize Health, Happiness, and Spiritual Well-Being.* New York: Penguin Random House, 2013.

Cuddy, Amy Joy. *Presence: Bringing Your Boldest Self to Your Biggest Challenges.* New York: Little, Brown Spark, 2018.

Glaser, Judith E. *Conversational Intelligence: How Great Leaders Build Trust and Get Extraordinary Results*. Philadelphia: Taylor & Francis, 2016.

Guo, Xueqi. "Unreliable Memory: It Makes Things Up." Psych 256: Cognitive Psychology FA 15. Penn State, November 22, 2015. Blog post. https://sites.psu.edu/psych256fa15/2015/11/22/unreliable-memory-it-makes-things-up/comment-page-1/.

Hanson, Rick. "Your Wonderful Brain." Wise Brain, 2007. https://s3-us-west-1.amazonaws.com/fwb-media.rickhanson.net/PDFfiles/YourWonderfulBrain.pdf.

Hogenboom, Melissa. "Why Does the Human Brain Create False Memories?" BBC News, September 29, 2013. https://www.bbc.com/news/science-environment-24286258

Madanes, Cloe. "The 6 Human Needs for Fulfillment." CloeMadanes.com. October 12, 2016. Blog post. https://cloemadanes.com/2016/10/12/the-6-human-needs-for-fulfillment/.

Robbins, Anthony, and Cloé Madanes. "Core 100 Training." Robbins Madanes Training. Lecture presented at the Core 100 Training, 2016. https://rmtcenter.com/core100now/

Ruiz, Don Miguel. *The Four Agreements: A Toltec Wisdom Book*. Toltec Wisdom Series. Carlsbad, CA: Hay House Inc., 1997.

About the Author

Karen Pohlman is the unmessable mindset mentor for female leaders everywhere who realize that life is short and it's time to get equipped to shine their light in the world!

Her own struggles in her marriage and the loss of her home and business in the 2008 global financial crisis led her on a seventeen-year journey of personal development. That journey included a certification in strategic intervention coaching and a collection of her lessons on resilience that have been incorporated into her new book, *Be Unmessable.*

Karen shows readers how to create a unique, personalized process for facing any stressful situation, conversation, or crisis. She equips them to do that without losing a lot of time wrapped up in trying to "figure it out" on the fly and while obtaining more of what they really want in life.

She is an entrepreneur, mom to three amazing humans and lives with her talented business partner and husband, along with their two beautiful dogs, in the Old West sunny town of San Jose, New Mexico.

Find her at karenpohlman.com

Instagram: @beunmessable

Facebook: Karen Palin Pohlman

Invite Karen to your book club: Karen@anotherway.live

Made in the USA
Middletown, DE
17 January 2022